What Oth...

Fear God and Keep His Commandments

IN THIS BRIEF BUT SENSITIVE COMMENTARY ON ECCLESIASTES, RATA and Roberts highlight the biblical book's revelation concerning personal and social tensions people face in a fallen world. Instead of placing the emphasis on self-help or some sort of human reformation through psychiatry, the authors focus on the sovereignty of God and the authority of His Word. Throughout the volume the authors explain the psychological perspectives that Ecclesiastes reveals—perspectives that call for the necessity of God's work through His Word for changing lives. Thus exposition leads to a consideration of the implications of the text for the daily struggles of life "under the sun."

William D. Barrick
Professor of Old Testament and Director of Th.D. Studies
The Master's Seminary

IT IS A PLEASURE TO COMMEND THIS NEW COMMENTARY ON ECCLESIASTES by Drs. Tiberius Rata and Kevin Roberts. It is a special joy because they make a great case for Solomonic authorship and they see the work as a positive message. It would be wonderful if the text of Ecclesiastes were read and reflected on more frequently in the Church and the culture around us.

Dr. Walter C. Kaiser Jr.
President Emeritus
Gordon-Conwell Theological Seminary

THE BOOK OF ECCLESIASTES IS DIFFICULT, BUT PROVIDES GREAT INSIGHT into our human condition. Is there meaning or purpose to life? Where is it to be found? Tiberius Rata, a biblical scholar, and Kevin

Roberts, a behavioral scientist, combine their skills to explore this profound book of wisdom. They not only open up the meaning of the book in its ancient context, they explore the significance of its message for our lives today. I recommend this book for all who want to seriously consider the true meaning of life.

Tremper Longman III
Robert H. Gundry Professor of Biblical Studies
Westmont College

HAVING KNOWN KEVIN ROBERTS FROM THE VERY BEGINNING OF HIS WALK with Christ, it brings heartfelt excitement to see him co-author this fine commentary on Ecclesiastes. In our present age of skepticism and futility, how important it is to take a fresh look at God's truth, knowing that there are indeed biblical answers to life's most challenging questions. Especially appreciated is the very first footnote in the book: "The authors presuppose the inerrancy of Scripture and that the Bible is God's Word, thus it contains accurate information (on) science and theology."

Keith Miller
Professor of Bible and Theology
Calvary Bible College

THE BOOK OF ECCLESIASTES INVITES THIS KIND OF COMMENTARY PER-haps more than any other book in the Bible: a mix of biblical exposition and psychological reflection. Tiberius Rata's running commentary through the book does a fine job of keeping the reader focused on the personal realities and reflections of "the preacher." Along the way, Kevin Roberts gives special attention to what is happening psychologically, even introducing various kinds of psychological theories where he sees them as applicable. Both writers deal sensitively with realities of our human existence and what it means to pursue the Lord in the midst of it all.

Richard E. Averbeck
Professor of Old Testament and Semitic Languages
Trinity Evangelical Divinity School

ECCLESIASTES HAS OFTEN BEEN OVERLOOKED IN THE PUBLICATION OF Old Testament commentaries, but this is corrected, in part, by the appearance of this fine volume. Solomon is the proposed author and his heart and life are the focus of special analysis. The social, ethical, and theological character of Ecclesiastes is handled with clarity and reliability. Its practical applications make this book a valuable tool in the hands of all audiences.

John J. Davis
President Emeritus and
Professor of Old Testament Studies
Grace Theological Seminary

FEAR GOD

and Keep
His Commandments

FEAR GOD

and Keep His Commandments

A PRACTICAL
EXPOSITION OF
ECCLESIASTES

BY TIBERIUS RATA
AND KEVIN ROBERTS

BMH BOOKS
P. O. BOX 544
WINONA LAKE, INDIANA 46590
BMHBOOKS.COM

Fear God and Keep His Commandments
A Practical Exposition of Ecclesiastes

Copyright © Tiberius Rata and Kevin Roberts, 2016

ISBN: 978-0-88469-299-7
RELIGION / Bible / Ecclesiastes

Published by BMH Books, Winona Lake, IN 46590
bmhbooks.com

Printed in the United States of America

Acknowledgements

My study of Ecclesiastes has taken me on a long journey, down many unmarked roads and rabbit trails. Along this journey, I have found myself seeking to learn the answers to many of life's questions. Instead, I realize there is no end to this journey. With each fork in the road, there are so many mysteries, incomprehensible to the finite human mind. It is with deep appreciation that I thank my wife, Heather, and our children, Isaac and Rachel, whose patience and love are truly God's blessing. I cannot express my appreciation enough for those who have mentored me along the road, including Dr. Keith Miller, Dr. David Plaster, and Dr. Tom Edgington. I also would like to thank my good friends Dr. Tiberius Rata and Dr. Joe Graham, who patiently listened to me explain my unformed thoughts. To all of these people I express my limitless gratitude as we spend our time on earth together and live out Ecclesiastes 4:12: "And though a man might prevail against one who is alone, two will withstand him—a threefold cord is not quickly broken."

Kevin

I dedicate this work to my beautiful and wonderful wife, Carmen, who has always been very supportive of my work. She is indeed a gift from the LORD (Proverbs 18:22; 19:14). We have been blessed with two amazing children who love the LORD and who are growing more and more in the grace and knowledge of our LORD and Savior Jesus Christ. Timothy and Nicholas, may you always find fulfillment in a close relationship to God the Creator and Sustainer of all.

I also want to thank my friend and colleague, Mark Soto, who helps me to think theologically and systematically. He teaches me to love the Word of God but most of all, to love the God of the Word.

Finally, I want to thank Kevin for being a great friend and a godly example of humility. You embody what it means to love God with both heart and mind. When I grow up, I want to be like you!

Tiberius

WE WANT TO THANK TERRY WHITE FOR ASKING US TO DO THIS PROJECT, Liz Gates for her patience, and Jesse Deloe for his very competent and thorough work of editing. May the Good Lord richly reward all of you!

Kevin and Tiberius
Winona Lake, Indiana
April 2016

Table of Contents

Introduction

THIS INTERDISCIPLINARY COMMENTARY IS WRITTEN FOR THOSE WHO want to study the Bible from a conservative theological position. This includes pastors, professors, Sunday School teachers, and laypeople who want both a theological and psychological perspective on this much beloved and fascinating Old Testament book.[1]

Authorship and Date

The book of Ecclesiastes was written by Solomon, Israel's third king. Even though his name does not appear, his literary and contextual fingerprints are all over the book.[2] The book starts by identifying the author, "The words of Qoheleth, the son of David, king in Jerusalem" (1:1). While the word "son" can refer to a descendent of David, not necessarily a biological son, verse 12 clarifies the fact that the son is none other than Solomon. "I, Qoheleth, have been king over

---

1 The authors presuppose the inerrancy of Scripture and that the Bible is God's Word, thus it contains accurate information regarding all matters including science and theology.

2 Even if Solomon's name would have been mentioned in 1:1 and/or 1:12, some scholars still would have rejected the book's Solomonic authorship. This is clear from the way they deal with the authorship of the Song of Songs where even though Solomon's name does appear, many scholars reject the claim that Solomon wrote the book. A few scholars who accept Solomonic authorship of Ecclesiastes are Bill Barrick, Duane Garrett, and Walter Kaiser.

Israel in Jerusalem" (1:12). The only son of David that ruled over Israel in Jerusalem was Solomon. After Solomon's death the kingdom was divided into the Northern and Southern Kingdoms, so David's descendants that ruled in Jerusalem ruled over Judah (the Southern Kingdom) not Israel (the Northern Kingdom). Thus, the book can be dated around 940-932 B.C.[3]

Arguments against Solomonic authorship have been made on linguistic grounds. Delitzsch famously affirmed that "if the Book of Koheleth were of old Solomonic origin, then there is no history of the Hebrew language."[4] Others followed and affirmed that the presence of Aramaisms in the book suggest that the book was written at a later date. Zoeckler suggested that Aramaisms were present in almost every verse, Delitzsch found about ninety-six, while Hengstenberg found only ten.[5] The inconsistency of such scholarship has led more modern scholars to conclude that that "the language of the book is not a certain barometer of date."[6]

Those who reject the claim that Solomon wrote the book also cite internal evidence. Referring to Ecclesiastes 4:1-3, Longman asks, "How could Solomon write these verses? He was the mightiest ruler of the land. He could easily have done more than bemoan the plight of the oppressed; he could have taken steps to alleviate it."[7] The assumption is that if Solomon is the king writing about problems in his kingdom, he would have done something about it. Longman goes on to suggest that Solomon "created a heavy burden for his people." But all this is not evidence for or against authorship. You can blame Solomon for being insensitive if you want, but that does not prove that he didn't write the book. If Solomon didn't write the book, it would be impossible to interpret the Bible correctly since knowing its historical milieu is imperative to understanding the message of the book.

---

3 William D. Barrick, *Ecclesiastes: The Philippians of the Old Testament* (Fearn, Ross-shire, Scotland: Christian Focus, 2011), 21.

4 Franz Delitzsch, *Song of Songs and Ecclesiastes,* translated by M.G. Easton (Grand Rapids: Eerdmans, 1970), 190.

5 Gleason L. Archer, *A Survey of Old Testament Introduction* (Chicago: Moody, 1994), 529.

6 Tremper Longman, *The Book of Ecclesiastes* (Grand Rapids: Eerdmans, 1998), 15.

7 Ibid., 6.

Theology: What Ecclesiastes teaches us about God

The Bible is a book about God, thus Ecclesiastes is a book about God. God is not Deus Absconditus, the hidden god, but rather He reveals Himself through His Word, even through this fascinating book of Ecclesiastes. Solomon was not an atheist. God inspired him through the Holy Spirit, and He also appeared to Him twice (1 Kings 3:5, 9:2). For Solomon, God is the Sovereign God in charge of both history and humanity (1:13; 2:26; 3:11, 14; 5:18-20; 6:1-2; 7:14; 8:15; 9:1). There is no hint of evolution in the book because God is the Creator (3:11, 14; 7:29; 8:16-17; 11:5; 12:1ff). "Remember also your Creator" is Solomon's exhortation toward the end of the book. God created humanity at the beginning of history, and He will judge humanity at the end (3:17; 5:4, 6; 8:12-13; 11:9; 12:14). Solomon presents God as eternal (3:11, 14; 12:5, 7), holy (5:4; 7:29), omnipresent, omniscient, and omnipotent (5:2, 6; 7:13; 8:16-17; 11:5; 12:14). Because of who He is, God should be feared (3:14; 5:7; 8:12-13; 12:13) and obeyed (5:1-7; 8:2; 12:1, 13).

Ecclesiastes 1

1:1-2
Qoheleth and his refrain

1:3-11
Qoheleth and his interpretation of time and the world

1:12-18
Qoheleth and his view of wisdom

1:1-2 Qoheleth and his refrain

1:1 The words of the Preacher, the son of David, king in Jerusalem.

The first verse introduces us to the author, Solomon, the son of David, the third king of Israel.[1] Internal and external evidence point to Solomon as the author of the book. Verse 12 clarifies this since Solomon was the only son of David who ruled over Israel in Jerusalem. After Solomon's death God split the kingdom in half, with the descendants of David ruling over Judah in Jerusalem. The northern

---

1 Solomonic authorship of Ecclesiastes was generally accepted until the 19th century. While scholars have cited the language of the book as a barometer for the date, these scholars disagree even what an Aramaism is. For example, Zoeckler affirms that Aramaisms appear in almost every verse while Delitzsch lists 96 such instances. Hengstenberg, on the other hand, finds only five Aramaisms in the entire book. It is clear then that what drives the non-Solomonic authorship movement is not language but motivation that lies elsewhere. See Gleason L. Archer, *A Survey of Old Testament Introduction* (Chicago: Moody, 1994), 528-530. See also Cristian Rata, "Sweet and Lawful Delights: Puritan Interpretation of Ecclesiastes," in *The Words of the Wise are Like Goads: Engaging Qohelet in the 21st Century*, edited by Mark Boda, Tremper Longman, and Cristian Rata (Winona Lake, IN: Eisenbrauns, 2013), 69-86.

kingdom of Israel had its capital first at Shechem and later in Samaria. The book affirms that the author had great wisdom (1:16), he undertook massive building projects (2:4-6), he was wealthy (2:7-8), and he had a large harem (2:8). This is consistent with the description of Solomon given in 1 Kings. Rabbinic tradition also points to Solomonic authorship of the book. The first chapter of the Targum to Qoheleth says, "When Solomon King of Israel foresaw, by the spirit of prophecy that the kingdom of Rehoboam his son would be divided with Jeroboam the son of Nebat, that Jerusalem and the holy temple would be destroyed, and that the people of Israel would be exiled, he said by the divine word, 'Vanity of vanities is this world! Vanity of vanities is all which I and my father David strived for.'"[2]

Parallels between 1 Kings and Ecclesiastes

Similarities	1 Kings	Ecclesiastes
Great wisdom	4:29-34	1:16; 2:9
Building projects	7:1; 9:10	2:4-6
Large harem	11:1-8	2:8
Unequaled wealth	10:14-29	2:7-8

The word translated "Preacher," is the Hebrew word qōhélet̲ which can be translated preacher, collector (of sentences), convener, leader or speaker of an assembly.[3] The term Ecclesiastes, came into English through the Septuagint (LXX), the Greek translation of the Old Testament. This term does fit Solomon's résumé as 1 Kings 4:32 affirms that Solomon "spoke 3,000 proverbs, and his songs were 1,005."

---

2 *The Targum to the Five Megillot: Ruth, Ecclesiastes, Canticles, Lamentations, Esther.* Codex Vatican Urbinati I (Jerusalem: Makor, 1977), 47.

3 BDB, tlhq, HALOT, tlhq. The word appears in this form only in Ecclesiastes 1:1, 2, 12; 7:27; 12:9, 10. The verb form appears in about 160 verses throughout the Old Testament.

1:2 "Completely meaningless," says the Preacher.
"Completely meaningless! Everything is meaningless."

Solomon comes to the end of his life, and looking back, he concludes, "Everything is meaningless." The word translated "meaningless" is the Hebrew word hébel which can be translated breath, vapor, vanity, or meaningless.[4] Job uses the word to describe the brevity of his life (Job 7:16), to describe working in vain (Job 9:29), to describe the emptiness of his friends' words (Job 21:34), and to refer to his friends' significance (Job 27:12). It could be that Solomon heard his father use the word as he composed the songs we know as Psalms. Indeed, David sang about the hébel nature (Psalm 39:5, 7) and the brevity of one's life (Psalm 39:12; 62:9).

The expression "completely meaningless" is literally "meaninglessness of meaninglessness."[5] This is not the perspective God wants His followers to have. This is not the perspective of a follower of Christ today. Solomon's refrain comes at the end of his life after he systematically and consistently disobeyed God. His perspective is from "under the sun" and from among his harem. God appeared to Solomon twice, but in God's communication with Solomon there were some very important "if" clauses: "...if you will walk in my ways..." (1 Kings 3:14), "...if you walk in my statutes and obey my rules and keep all my commandments and walk in them..." (1 Kings 6:12), "...if you walk before me as David your father walked..." (1 Kings 9:4). Solomon's disobedience started with a brilliant military move by marrying the daughter of Pharaoh (1 Kings 3:1). And while

---

4 D.C. Fredericks, "lb,h," in *The New International Dictionary of Old Testament Theology and Exegesis* (Grand Rapids: Zondervan, 1997), edited by Willem A. VanGemeren, 1005-1006. The word appears 38 times in Ecclesiastes and some scholars choose to translate the first word(s) of verse 2 "meaningless" (Longman, 59-64), "futile and fleeting" (Thomas Krüger, *Qoheleth: A Commentary* [Minneapolis: Fortress, 2004, 42], "absurd" (Fox, *A Time to Tear Down and a Time to Build Up: A Rereading of Ecclesiastes* [Grand Rapids, Eersmans, 1999], 35), "vanity" (Roland Murphy, Ecclesiastes, WBC 23A [Dallas: Thomas Nelson, 1992] 3) and even "utterly enigmatic" (Bartholomew, 101).

5 Longman, *Ecclesiastes*, 61. This expression is translated "vanity of vanities" in the KJV but that translation is misleading since vanity has to do with self-pride whereas in the context of the book, Solomon uses the word to refer to the emptiness he experiences away from the LORD.

that might have been strategic from a military perspective, Solomon's action was a direct act of rebellion against God who commanded the Israelites not to intermarry with pagan nations. Furthermore,

> King Solomon loved many foreign women, along with the daughter of Pharaoh: Moabite, Ammonite, Edomite, Sidonian, and Hittite women, from the nations concerning which the LORD had said to the people of Israel, "You shall not enter into marriage with them, neither shall they with you, for surely they will turn away your heart after their gods." Solomon clung to these in love (1 Kings 11:1-2).

The meaninglessness Solomon experienced is reserved for those who rebel against God. It is not the perspective of a Christ-follower who obeys God and serves Him wholeheartedly.

1:3-11 Qoheleth and his interpretation of time and the world

1:3 What does man gain by all the toil at which he toils under the sun?

Solomon's question suggests several implications. First, Solomon expects that people will toil. Second, Solomon expects that people will gain something from their toil. Third, this toil happens "under the sun." The same form of the word "gain" is used four other times in Ecclesiastes, and it always refers to gain, profit, or advantage.[6] The word translated "toil" is a key word throughout the book, appearing 35 times both as a verb and as a noun. The word is not unique to wisdom literature but appears in the Pentateuch, in the historical books, in the poetical books, as well as the prophets and can be translated toil, labor, or trouble.[7] All this toil is done "under the sun." At that time, there were three religious classes of people: the priests, the prophets, and the sages. The priests were concerned with things pertaining to the Temple. The prophets were mediators between God and humanity, communicating God's message (usually)

---

6 Ecclesiastes 1:3; 2:11, 13; 3:9; 5:1; 10:11.

7 Gen 41:51, Judg 10:16; Job 3:10; Psalm 25:18; Isa 10:1; Jer 20:18.

in a time of crisis. The sages were observing what was happening "under the sun." This expression occurs only in Ecclesiastes where it appears 29 times. Longman suggests that the expression "highlights the restricted scope of his inquiry,[8] an inquiry which is restricted to the earth. The Chronicler does tell us that Solomon wrote about things he observed "under the sun." Indeed, Solomon wrote about trees, beasts, birds, and reptiles (1 Kings 4:33). Solomon's rhetorical question implies the answer "Nothing," an answer which he will illustrate in the following verses.

1:4 A generation goes, and a generation comes, but the earth remains forever.

The word translated "generation" appears only here in Ecclesiastes but is a very common word appearing in the Torah, the Prophets, and the Writings.[9] Here, Solomon uses it to contrast the transient nature of humanity with the unmovable, constant nature of the earth. The 4th century theologian Jerome of Stridonium noted the irony present in this verse, "What is more vain than this vanity: that the earth, which was made for humans, stays—but humans themselves, the lords of the earth, suddenly dissolve into the dust?"[10] Recent scholars suggest that the word "generation" can refer both to humans and to the natural cycles. Crenshaw asserts that "the word dôr...suggests both nature and people...lending immense irony to the observation that the stage on which the human drama is played outlasts the actors themselves."[11]

---

8 Longman, Ecclesiastes, 66.

9 Some examples are: Gen 7:1; Exod 1:6; Num 32:13; Deut 1:35; Josh 11:2; Judges 1:27, 2:10; Psalm 12:7; Prov 27:24; Isa 13:20; Jer 2:31; Joel 1:3. Contra Ogden, Fox suggests that the word is best translated "generation" and not "cycle." See Michael V. Fox, "Qohelet 1:4," in JSOT 40 (1988),109 and Graham S. Ogden, "The Interpretation of rwd in Ecclesiastes 1.4," in JSOT 34 (1986):91-92.

10 As cited in Longman, *Ecclesiastes*, 67.

11 James L. Crenshaw, *Ecclesiastes*. OTL (Philadelphia: Westminster, 1987), 62.

> *1:5 The sun rises, and the sun goes down,*
> *and hastens to the place where it rises.*

Solomon's observations regarding things "under the sun" lead him to consider the sun itself. His geocentric view is consistent with the Ancient Near Eastern view that the sun went "under the earth and around to its place of rising."[12] The verb translated "hastens" can be used both in a positive or a negative sense. Longman notes that used positively, "the word means to pant with eagerness or desire," while negatively it means "to pant with exhaustion (like a woman in childbirth in Isaiah 42:14)."[13]

> *1:6 The wind blows to the south and goes around to the north;*
> *around and around goes the wind, and on its circuits the wind returns.*

While the wind can blow from the east/west and west/east, Solomon mentions only the south/north movement. This is not meant as a comprehensive, meteorological treatment of the wind movements, but rather a continuation of Solomon's argument of the monotony and meaninglessness of life.

> *1:7 All streams run to the sea, but the sea is not full;*
> *to the place where the streams flow, there they flow again.*

The cyclical motion of water might lead some to worship the Creator for His masterful design. This is not the case here where the author uses an observable feature of creation to argue for the futility and monotony of creation.[14]

> *1:8 All things are full of weariness; a man cannot utter it; the eye*
> *is not satisfied with seeing, nor the ear filled with hearing.*

---

12 Roland Murphy, *Ecclesiastes*, 7.

13 Longman, *Ecclesiastes*, 69.

14 Whybray affirms that verses 5-7 do not talk about futility or meaninglessness but rather they affirm the "unchanging character of natural phenomena." See R. N. Whybray, "Ecclesiastes 1:5-7 and the Wonders of Nature," in JSOT 41 (1988):105-112.

Even though Solomon, as the wisest man on earth, has a wide vocabulary at his disposal, he is at a loss for words when it comes to explaining the weariness of the monotonous aspects of life outlined above. The word translated "wearisome" is an adjective that appears also in Deuteronomy 25:18 and 2 Samuel 17:2 with the same meaning. Garrett writes, "Humans, confronted by the monotony and aimlessness of the situation in which they have been placed, have nothing to say."[15] Throughout the book, Qoheleth tries to use words to explain things (12:9-10), but now no such words are powerful or accurate enough. Qoheleth sees things as meaningless because they do not satisfy. Solomon saw many things, and yet his eyes were not satisfied. Solomon heard many things, and yet his ears were not satisfied. Godless endeavors, no matter how good they may appear, will never satisfy. They did not satisfy Solomon, and they still don't satisfy modern-day Solomons who try to find satisfaction apart from a correct relationship with God.

> *1:9-10 What has been is what will be, and what has been done is what will be done, and there is nothing new under the sun. Is there a thing of which it is said, "See, this is new"? It has been already in the ages before us.*

It is obvious that Solomon does not talk about technological advances, but rather about universal matters that he covers in the book, namely, birth, death, marriage, war, sunrise and sunset. While technological advances such as the automobile, wireless smart phones, and satellite TV have helped us in our quest for knowledge, we still are born and live under the sun, and we die, just like those who lived in Solomon's time. The rhetorical question, "Is there a thing of which it is said, 'See, this is new?'" is sandwiched between the answers, "What has been is what will be..." and "it has been already in the ages before us." Instead of standing in awe of the Creator God who sustains the universe, Solomon continues to revel in his pessimism.

---

15 Duane Garrett, *Proverbs, Ecclesiastes, Song of Songs*, NAC (Nashville: Broadman, 1993), 287.

1:11 There is no remembrance of former things, nor will there be any remembrance of later things yet to be among those who come after.

"The best is yet to come" was not part of Solomon's philosophical framework. If things were bad in the past, one can expect more of the same in the future. Is Solomon singing "an unhappy lament of a disappointed soul which has been dealt some rough blows by life"?[16] There is no doubt that the tone that he sets in the book is primarily pessimistic, but that is because he chose to consistently and systematically disobey God. The lesson must be learned: apart from a correct relationship with God, everything will be meaningless. Solomon stands as a monument to all those who try to fill the God-shaped void of their lives with something else rather than God.

1:12-18 Qoheleth and his view of wisdom

1:12 I, Qoheleth, have been king over Israel in Jerusalem.

We are reminded that the Preacher, the Teacher, is none other than Israel's third king, Solomon, the son of David (1:1). The use of the perfect tense of the verb "to be" does not mean that Solomon used to be king and that he is not a king anymore.[17] It also does not mean that Solomon is dead or that someone else is impersonating him.[18] After Solomon's death, the kingdom was divided, so the only son (or descendent) of David who ruled over Israel in Jerusalem was Solomon.

---

16 H.C. Leupold, *Exposition of Ecclesiastes* (Grand Rapids: Baker, 1952), 49.

17 The qal, perfect, 1cs of hyh can indicate completed action in the past, but the same form is used to denote the present tense or the present perfect (Gen 32:11; Exod 2:22; Ruth 1:12; Job 11:4; 30:9, 29; Ps 31:11; 69:9; 102:7; Prov 5:14; Jer 20:7; 23:9). Scholars who reject Solomonic authorship cannot do it based on the language of the book. Tremper Longman affirms, "My conclusion is that the language of the book is not a certain barometer of date." See Longman, *Ecclesiastes*, 15.

18 Generally speaking, scholars who reject Solomonic authorship of Ecclesiastes also reject the inerrancy of Scripture (there are exceptions of course). See Thomas Krüger, *Qoheleth*, 40, 62.

*1:13 And I set my heart to seek and to search out by wisdom all
that is done under heaven. It is a grievous task that God has given
to the children of man with which to be afflicted.*

Three times in the book Solomon "sets his heart" to do, seek, apply, or know. Here and in 8:16, he set his heart to seek and search
wisdom, while in 8:9 his heart "was set" to see all that was done under the sun. Throughout the book Solomon employs three different
verbs to indicate his multi-faceted search. Most often though, he
doesn't seem to find what he is looking for, or at least, he finds something that is not encouraging. His findings here suggest that God
afflicts people with "a grievous task," and yet we are not clearly told
what this task is. It could be that "all that is done under heaven" is a
grievous task (unhappy business), or it could be that the search for
wisdom is ultimately a frustrating, hopeless task. Fox explains, "The
search for understanding may be frustrated, but it is not wrong or in
violation of God's will. On the contrary, this is something God wants
humans do and has, in fact, imposed on them."[19]

*1:14 I have seen everything that is done under the sun, and behold,
everything is meaningless, and a striving after wind.*

Solomon repeats the refrain that is first mentioned in verse 2, but this
time he utters it after he saw "everything that is done under the sun."
His conclusion is not a result of divine revelation, but the result of
personal reflection. Whether the phrase "everything is meaningless"
refers to "intellectual labor,"[20] an ironic summary statement,[21] or the
"transitory nature of human effort,"[22] it is clear that "the phrase rein-
forces the conclusion that life is hébel, meaningless."[23]

---

19 Michael V. Fox, *Ecclesiastes*, The JPS Bible Commentary (Philadelphia: Jewish
Publication Society, 2004), 9.

20 Garrett, *Proverbs, Ecclesiastes, Song of Songs*, 289.

21 C.L. Seow, *Ecclesiastes*, AB (New Haven: Yale, 1997), 146.

22 Fredericks and Estes, *Ecclesiastes and The Song of Songs*, 82.

23 Longman, *Ecclesiastes*, 82.

*1:15 What is crooked cannot be made straight,
and what is lacking cannot be counted.*

In Ecclesiastes 7:13 Solomon asks, "Who can straighten what He [God] has made crooked?" Here in 1:15 Solomon seems to resign himself to the fact that some wrongs cannot be made right. Could it be that he was influenced by Egyptian wisdom literature? Fox notes that "the Egyptian sage Anii uses the twisted stick as a metaphor for a foolish or perverse pupil who, he insists, can be educated: "The crooked stick left on the ground … if the carpenter takes it, he straightens it, makes of it a noble's staff."[24] Later, the rabbis proposed that "crooked" refers to "a sinful person or a corrupt deed, which cannot be corrected."[25]

The second part of the verse seems to be obvious: one cannot count what does not exist. Garrett suggests that what is "lacking" refers to "lack of information,"[26] Lohfink thinks it's referring to a farmer's "meager harvest,"[27] while Galling thinks that "originally it referred to the twisted back of an old man (15a), and the "missing" (15b) refers to the ensuing lack of height."[28] Whatever was meant here, Longman concludes that "the essentially flawed nature of the world is something self-evident and cannot be disputed."[29]

*1:16 I said in my heart, "I have acquired great wisdom,
surpassing all who were over Jerusalem before me, and my heart
has had great experience of wisdom and knowledge."*

Scripture corroborates Solomon's statement. In the book of 1 Kings we are told that Solomon received wisdom from God and that he gained knowledge of many things under the sun from plant life to

---

24 AEL 2.145 as cited by Michael V. Fox, *Ecclesiastes*, 9.

25 Fox, *Ecclesiastes*, 9.

26 Garrett, *Proverbs, Ecclesiastes, Song of Songs*, 289-290.

27 Norbert Lohfink, *Qoheleth* (Minneapolis: Fortress: 2003), 48. Seow agrees that it is an economic term that is opposite in meaning to surplus or gain. See Seow, *Ecclesiastes*, 123.

28 Murphy, *Ecclesiastes*, 13-14.

29 Longman, *Ecclesiastes*, 83.

animals and fish.[30] We are told in the historical books that Solomon did not obey God as David his father had done, but it was Solomon's estimation that his wisdom surpassed his father's, and it surpassed the wisdom of the Jebusites who preceded David. The comparison need not be with previous kings alone, but could include previous sages or other officials.

> *1:17 And I applied31 my heart to know wisdom and to know madness and folly. I perceived that this also is a striving after wind.*

The book of Proverbs tells us that folly is the opposite of wisdom. In this context it could be that Solomon tells us that he used his entire "range of human mental capabilities"[32] in his quest. As in verse 14, his search has proven fruitless.[33]

> *1:18 For in much wisdom is much grief, and he who increases knowledge increases sorrow.*

One might expect blessedness and joy as a result of pursuing wisdom and knowledge, but for Solomon that is not the case. Instead of joy and blessedness, he found grief and sorrow. Indeed, that will be the result of all those who pursue wisdom and knowledge apart from a correct relationship with God. The Bible dispels the myth that ignorance is bliss. Jesus taught us to learn from the birds of the air;[34] Peter exhorted us to "grow in the grace and knowledge of our Lord and

---

30 1 Kings 4:29-33.

31 The form "I set/gave/applied my heart" appears a few times in Ecclesiastes (1:13, 17; 8:16; 9:1).

32 Fox, *Ecclesiastes*, 10.

33 The expression "a striving after the wind" appears also in 2:11, 17; 26; 4:4, 6; 16; 6:9. Gordis proposes the following translation, "I said to myself, I have gotten great wisdom, over all who were before me over Jerusalem, and my heart has seen much wisdom and knowledge. And I applied my mind and learnt that wisdom and knowledge is madness and folly; I perceived that this too is vanity and a striving after wind. For in much wisdom is much vexation and he who increases knowledge increases sorrow." See Robert Gordis, "Ecclesiastes 1:17 – its Text and Interpretation," in *JBL* 56:3 (2013):323-330.

34 Matthew 6:26.

Savior Jesus Christ";[35] and Paul taught us to learn not to go beyond what is written.[36] Does God promise an abundant life absent from grief and sorrow? Never! But He does promise that His presence and power will be ours without exception. Thus, the follower of Christ, and the student of the Word (one and the same person) should not make this verse his/her life motto, but should rather seek to learn more of God and His world, accepting the fact that grief and sorrow will be part of the growing process.

Reflections from a psychological perspective

Solomon addresses the monotony and boredom that is associated with this life. He asserts in this first chapter that we must all learn to accept the monotony and the weariness of this life. He takes a tone of world-weariness and of someone who is struggling to resolve the mysteries of life under the sun. The following chapters often frustrate some readers because Solomon appears to be musing from topic to topic. At times he appears to be trying to resolve many of life's problems, such as death, money, time, and old age. As he struggles through many of these problems, he seems to jump from topic to topic as he finds the interrelatedness of these issues. There appear to be times when Solomon is engaging both sides of an issue and sharing both the human perspective and the ultimate answers given by God. Solomon also lays out a basic human problem: that mankind will never be satisfied in this life with what they see, feel, or hear. Solomon asserts that this life will never provide peace and contentment. Also, he illustrates that a hedonistic pursuit will provide only temporary pleasures, as pleasure-seeking behavior will ultimately lead to one's own unhappiness and destruction.

Solomon presents the case that mankind will go throughout this life and fail to accept that reality. Despite the overwhelming evidence to the contrary, mankind will experience a great desire to make life "under the sun" work on their terms to fulfill their needs and desires.

---

35 2 Peter 3:18.
36 1 Corinthians 4:6.

However, attempting to evade reality at all costs frequently results in mental health or spiritual problems. Solomon will keep reiterating throughout the book that whether it is wealth, wisdom, strong drink, or sexual pleasures, all of these strivings will fall horribly short. As we will see, escaping reality frequently has emotional, spiritual, physical, career, and even educational consequences. Solomon forewarns us that all these things have been tried before, and they did not work then, nor will they work today. He then proceeds to warn the readers that they can waste their lives in these pointless pursuits, but that it is impossible for mankind to find ultimate purpose and meaning in a finite world. Ultimate purpose and meaning cannot be discovered through knowledge or wisdom with finite minds in a finite world. Instead, we must seek the omniscient and omnipresent God who provides both meaning and purpose.

1:1-2

The initial sentiment expressed by Solomon regarding meaninglessness is not an uncommon assessment at this stage in his life. Some have hypothesized that Solomon may have written the book as part of a midlife crisis. Many other writers see this book as being written near the end of Solomon's life.[37] Psychologist Erik Erickson (1959) developed a series of what he termed Psychosocial Stages of human development.[38] These Psychosocial stages, Erickson believed, are stages that all humans experience over the course of their life. Erickson believed that human beings develop through the sum of their personal experiences and that their self-identity is based on the culmination of human interactions. The last of these psychosocial stages is titled Ego Integrity vs. Despair. According to Erickson, it is at this stage of life (approximately age 65) that people look back over their lives and begin to assess whether their lives were either misspent or marked by a sense of fulfillment. It was Erickson's belief that the accomplishments (toil) of man "under the sun" could provide mean-

---

37 William D. Barrick, *Ecclesiastes*, 16.

38 John W. Santrock, *Essentials of Life-Span Development*. Fourth edition. (New York, NY: McGraw-Hill, 2016). 393-394.

ing and purpose. Furthermore, he believed that if one accomplished enough, then he or she would be able to develop a sense of ego integrity and thus experience a general sense of well-being and wisdom in late life.[39] As one looks at Solomon's life and the book of Ecclesiastes, it appears that despite his many accomplishments, he never experienced this general sense of well-being that Erickson promised. The text makes it clear that Solomon surpassed all of Israel's previous kings in wealth, possessions, and wisdom (1 Kings 10:23). Despite his numerous accomplishments, it was his pursuit of these things that ultimately resulted in Solomon's horrible disappointment and boredom with everything "under the sun."

1:3-8

I believe that Ecclesiastes 1:8 sets up the entire problem of human striving from a psychological perspective. Solomon contends that the human soul will constantly experience restlessness, and the senseless pursuit of everything from pleasure to wisdom will not solve this dilemma (Ecc 1:8 and 3:11). The human soul will experience this restlessness because of our relentless efforts to fill our souls apart from God. Humans, though, continue to strive toward this end, despite the fact that it will never bring the ultimate satisfaction that man longs for. Instead, we attempt to use alcohol, food, money, and sex to provide temporary relief to our restless existence. The use of these false idols, intentionally or unintentionally, results in a pathological relationship with them. We end up trusting in these false idols to satisfy our restless spirit or painful existence. But in reality, these false idols will only leave us with emotional, spiritual, physical, and career-related consequences. Humans, though, will try to deny their restlessness, and attempt to numb the guilt and shame associated with the consequences of following false idols.

The Hedonistic pursuit of mankind promises that you will turn aside from God and seek pleasure, but this pursuit will bring ruin to your house (1 Kings 9:9). Solomon argues in verse 8 that mankind will experience a restlessness that will not be satisfied. As we will see

---

39 Ibid.

in later chapters, Solomon will describe the thoughts, behaviors, and consequences of turning aside from God and foolishly striving after false gods. This aimless, cyclical striving often leaves us dissatisfied and wondering if there is more to this life. Solomon's life was living proof that you can attain everything under the sun and experience the highest of pleasures, but that such attainment will never satisfy your soul. Ultimate answers under the sun do not exist, and in fact, this circular striving approach to life apart from God can lead us into utter despair. It is man's duty both to obey and to glorify God, but can man really do that while he seeks to find his meaning under the sun apart from God? Solomon with his great wisdom and resources was never able to attain meaning apart from God, and neither will we. God explains to Solomon in his second appearance to him in 1 Kings 9:3-9 what would be the consequences of allowing his heart to turn aside from him. However, Solomon was unable to heed this warning and his mind was not "wholly" devoted to God (1 Kings 11:4).

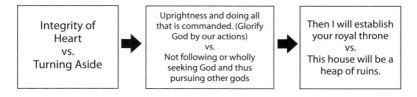

1:9-11

Solomon's persistent pessimism and dissatisfaction with life is evident is these verses as he illustrates that everything he searched for was just simply a variation of things already seen in generations past. His efforts to fill this God-shaped void in his soul were consistently unsuccessful. Solomon had all the financial resources, property, wives, and every other type of pleasure afforded to a King, and yet he could find no satisfaction or meaning in those things. Is it possible that Solomon is reflecting on his aimless wandering away from God, finding his heart weary, and feeling inexpressible emptiness? This emptiness is something each generation will experience despite renewed efforts to find the "new" things to satisfy the soul. In modern day culture it may come in the form of fitness, pornography, material possessions, or even drugs and alcohol. But these things are just the "new" substitutes that Satan uses to tempt the hearts of men away from the Lord of our lives. As an addiction counselor for many years, I found that when a person gives up his or her substance of choice, there is a grieving process that he or she will experience. This grieving process occurs when the person realizes that this false idol cannot and will not satisfy the soul and, in fact, is utterly destroying him or her spiritually, emotionally, and physically. Solomon's pessimism is likely due to his repeated unsuccessful efforts to look for meaning and purpose under the sun. Life has meaning and purpose only when we fear God, glorify Him, and place Him as the center of our attention instead of pursuing our false idols and substitutes under the sun.

1: 12-15

The first question from verse 13 is the complaint that Solomon seems to be raising with God. Is he blaming God for his own systematic disobedience and failure to show the humility of someone who has clearly disobeyed God's commands? Or is Solomon raising the question whether the system of Old Testament times was a paradigm that was in desperate need of revision? Is Solomon simply stating that sinful, broken people living in a fallen world are going to be prone to wander and not keep their eyes on God, as he himself had done? Saint Augustine warns that "the saints of God had their whole hope and aim centered on the everlasting good. Their whole desire pointed upward to the lasting and invisible realm, lest the love of what is visible drag them down to lower things."[40] Saint Augustine suggests that the lower things of this world will drag us down unless our lives are centered on God.

Solomon goes on to state that we cannot fix what is crooked. A counselor can help someone see the sinfulness of his choices and the consequences of his actions. Enabled by the Holy Spirit, the counselor can even help someone see the absolute need of a Savior. But this man or woman will still be a sinful, broken human being. No

---

40 Thomas À Kempis, *The Imitation of Christ* (Macon, GA: 2007), 25.

matter what is done in counseling or in the heart of a man, he will still be found crooked and lacking. Solomon illustrates clearly that the human condition is in desperate need of another solution to the restlessness of man, thus setting the stage for the entrance of Jesus Christ.

Ecclesiastes 2

2:1-7
Godless pleasures lead to emptiness

2:8-11
Godless relationships lead to bitterness

2:12-17
Godless knowledge leads to hatred of life

2:18-26
Godless work leads to lack of vision

2:1-7 Godless pleasures lead to emptiness

2:1 I said in my heart, "Come now, I will test you with pleasure; enjoy yourself." But behold, this also was vanity.

Solomon urges "himself into action"[1] by using the phrase, "I said in my heart," a phrase that occurs only in Ecclesiastes (2:1, 3:17, and 3:18). Apart from a correct relationship with God, Solomon does not find satisfaction, so he tries to fill his inner void with pleasure. "Enjoy yourself," is his command to himself. The following verses will explain how he pursued pleasure, but his conclusion, "This also was vanity," does not surprise the reader since it is consistent with Qoheleth's refrain, "Everything is meaningless; all is vanity."

---

1 Longman, *Ecclesiastes*, 88. Garrett sees the dialogue as an exaggerated poetry between Qoheleth and his personified heart. See Garrett, *Ecclesiastes*, 291.

2:2 I said of laughter, "It is mad," and of pleasure, "What use is it?"

Could laughter fill the void of one's heart? Not only did laughter not satisfy Solomon, he concluded "it is mad." The word translated "mad" can mean "foolish, blind," in other words, "not wise." Even though people in the United States spend 5 percent of their income on entertainment every year, they are still left empty and unfulfilled. Furthermore, pleasure also proves useless. Longman argues that "the force of the verse is to deny the possibility of meaning through pleasure."[2] Even if laughter and pleasure play a role in life, they do not give meaning or provide ultimate satisfaction, apart from a correct relationship with God.

2:3 I searched with my heart how to cheer my body with wine— my heart still guiding me with wisdom—and how to lay hold on folly, till I might see what was good for the children of man to do under heaven during the few days of their life.

Laughter and pleasure did not fulfill Solomon. Could wine do it? In his quest for meaning and satisfaction, Solomon hopes that if his body feels good, he will achieve his goal. The expression "my heart still guiding me with wisdom," suggests that he did not abuse alcohol, but was trying to achieve enjoyment through consumption. In other words, this is "a carefully controlled experiment."[3] And yet, he will conclude as before, that "all is vanity and striving after the wind" (v. 11). But what does Solomon mean by "lay hold on folly"? Some scholars suggest that he is trying "harmless and enjoyable forms of nonsense,"[4] material pleasures,[5] or "to explore pleasure as the world defines it and to drink its cup to the bottom to see if it does indeed provide meaning in life."[6] While he examines folly, he does not indulge in it. Nevertheless, his goal was "to see what was good for the

---

2 Longman, *Ecclesiastes*, 88.

3 Leupold, *Ecclesiastes*, 60.

4 Ibid.

5 Fox, *A Time to Tear Down and A Time to Build Up* (Grand Rapids: Eerdmans, 1999), 179.

6 Bartholomew, *Ecclesiastes*, 131.

children of man to do under heaven." Some years later, the prophet Micah will outline what was good, as far as God is concerned: "to do justice, to love kindness, and to walk humbly with your God" (Micah 6:8). Did Solomon succeed in what was good before God? His record shows that he did justice (1 Kings 3:16ff), but did he love kindness, or walk humbly with Yahweh? Could it be that it was the pride of his heart that led him to polygamy and idolatry? One thing is clear: so far, he is not satisfied or fulfilled in life. So his search continues.

2:4-7 I made great works. I built houses and planted vineyards for myself. I made myself gardens and parks, and planted in them all kinds of fruit trees. I made myself pools from which to water the forest of growing trees. I bought male and female slaves, and had slaves who were born in my house. I had also great possessions of herds and flocks, more than any who had been before me in Jerusalem.

Could work projects satisfy and fulfill Solomon? The houses, vineyards, gardens, parks, fruit trees, and pools still do not satisfy him, probably because these are not public works, but as he admits, they are "for myself" (v. 5). Indeed 1 Kings 7:1-12; 9:15; and 2 Chronicles 8:1-6 detail his building projects that span from Jerusalem to Megiddo to Hazor to Gezer. The reference to gardens, forests, and trees could lead one to think back to the Garden of Eden.[7] The phrase "all kinds of fruit trees" is very similar to the language of Genesis 1:11. Subsequently, Verheij suggests that "the passage can be read as referring to a failed attempt on the part of Qoheleth at creating something like Paradise."[8] Krüger has great insight when he states that Solomon "wastes no thought on the happiness or unhappiness of the people who contribute to his happiness and carry out his 'great works' for him."[9] Can we compare Solomon to today's workaholic

---

7 Verheij suggests that 2:4-6 "not only refers to royal parks as the Solomonic ones described in the book of Kings. It also contains allusions to the Creation Narrative, especially to the Garden of Eden." See Arian J.C. Verheij, "Paradise Retried: on Qohelet 2:4-6," in *JSOT* 50 (1991), 113-115.

8 A.J.C. Verheij, ibid.

9 Krüger, *Qoheleth*, 66.

who is told that the only way to live is by working 24/7 and by burning the candle at both ends? Solomon had no proverbial ladder to climb, and yet he indulged in all these projects only to leave him just as empty, because his problem was not on the outside but on the inside.

Solomon's unprecedented wealth required a large number of servants. Some of them were purchased and some were born from slaves that were already working on his estate. In a primarily agrarian society, one's wealth was calculated also in the number of cattle he possessed. We are not given a number, as in the case of Job, but the herds and flocks are labeled as "great." Solomon says, "I am rich; no, richer than anyone who lived before me in Jerusalem."[10] And yet, these riches, apart from a correct relationship with God, did not fulfill or satisfy Solomon. So, his search continues.

2:8-11 *Godless relationships lead to bitterness*

> 2:8 *I also gathered for myself silver and gold and the treasure of kings and provinces. I got singers, both men and women, and many concubines, the delight of the sons of man.*

It is no secret that, by any standard, Solomon was a rich man. His wealth is summarized in the historical books and included gold gathered from business deals, a fleet of ships, chariots, and imported horses from Egypt (1 Kings 10:14-29). Like his father David, Solomon enjoyed choral music. While the Levitical choir would have been a men's choir, Solomon's choir is formed by both men and women singers. Thus, this is no cultic choir performing at the temple, but one that entertains Solomon. In his search for pleasure, Solomon seeks sexual pleasure, but not in the way God ordained in the Garden of Eden. Solomon's self-made Garden of Eden has no forbidden trees, so he has "many concubines." Indeed, 1 Kings 11:1-3 summarizes Solomon's demise.

---

10 Before his father David moved the capital from Hebron to Jerusalem, the city was inhabited by the Jebusites. Furthermore, Melchizedek (Gen 14:18), Adonizedek (Josh 10:1), and Araunah (2 Sam 24:23) also ruled from Jerusalem.

Now King Solomon loved many foreign women, along with the daughter of Pharaoh: Moabite, Ammonite, Edomite, Sidonian, and Hittite women, from the nations concerning which the LORD had said to the people of Israel, "You shall not enter into marriage with them, neither shall they with you, for surely they will turn away your heart after their gods." Solomon clung to these in love. He had 700 wives, who were princesses, and 300 concubines. And his wives turned away his heart.

Even though these concubines are considered in the world's eyes as "the delight of the sons of man," they are not so in the eyes of the Creator of the sons of man. "The LORD was angry with Solomon" for his departure from Yahweh's law (1 Kings 11:9). Thus, just because something is culturally acceptable does not mean it is God-approved. Did illicit sexual pleasure fulfill Solomon? No, it did not. But he bought Satan's lies, just as many do today. Why doesn't illicit sexual pleasure satisfy and fulfill? Because it is not God's design. His design was drawn back in the Garden of Eden, one man and one woman in relationship with each other and both in relationship with their Creator.

2:9-11 So I became great and surpassed all who were before me in Jerusalem. Also my wisdom remained with me. And whatever my eyes desired I did not keep from them. I kept my heart from no pleasure, for my heart found pleasure in all my toil, and this was my reward for all my toil. Then I considered all that my hands had done and the toil I had expended in doing it, and behold, all was vanity and a striving after wind, and there was nothing to be gained under the sun.

Repeating his claim from verse 3, Solomon considers himself superior to those who ruled before him in Jerusalem. Some leaders fall due to moral failure and some fall because of pride. Solomon failed in both. Neither humility nor self-control was precious and a necessary commodity in his life. Even so, Solomon maintains that he remained wise even though he indulged in pleasure. The fact that he exercised no restraint suggests that he was building for himself a Garden of Eden but with no forbidden trees. And yet, the results are anticlimactic. "All was vanity and striving after wind," is his well-known refrain. Why does he find no satisfaction? Because he consistently and systematically disobeys God's Law. And one cannot find satisfaction or fulfillment apart from a correct relationship with God. The LORD says to Moses,

> Speak to the people of Israel, and tell them to make tassels on the corners of their garments throughout their generations, and to put a cord of blue on the tassel of each corner. And it shall be a tassel for you to look at and remember all the commandments of the LORD, to do them, not to follow after your own heart and your own eyes, which you are inclined to whore after (Numbers 15:38-39).

The result of Solomon's rebellion is emptiness, striving after wind. As Garrett notes, "the payoff did not match the effort expended."[11] More than that, Solomon will affirm that "more bitter than death [is] the woman whose heart is snares and nets, and whose hands are fetters" (Ecc 7:26). It is a timeless lesson for all to learn that godless relationships disappoint, leave one empty, and lead to bitterness.

2:12-17 Godless knowledge leads to hatred of life

So I turned to consider wisdom and madness and folly. For what can the man do who comes after the king? Only what has already been done. Then I saw that there is more gain in wisdom than in folly, as there is more gain in light than in darkness. The wise person has his eyes in his head, but the fool walks in darkness. And yet I perceived that the same event happens to all of them. Then I said in my heart, "What happens to the fool will happen to me also. Why then have I been so very wise?" And I said in my heart that this also is vanity. For of the wise as of the fool there is no enduring remembrance, seeing that in the days to come all will have been long forgotten. How the wise dies just like the fool! So I hated life, because what is done under the sun was grievous to me, for all is vanity and a striving after wind.

---

11 Garrett, *Ecclesiastes*, 292.

The pleasures of the flesh did not satisfy Solomon, so now the king turns to compare and contrast wisdom, madness, and folly.[12] Even though there is an element of pessimism in his question and answer, "For what can the man do who comes after the king? Only what has already been done," he does conclude that wisdom is superior to folly. And the difference is like day and night, light and darkness. Thus, one will be able to clearly see and know that the wise sees while the fool walks in darkness. And yet, there is still a sense of fatalism that lingers as Solomon states, "the same event happens to all of them." The common fate of death is what renders things meaningless for Solomon, and for those who pursue satisfaction and meaning apart from a correct relationship with God. Solomon implies that the wise deserves something better, but in light of Genesis 3, death is the direct consequence of being sinful beings.[13]

In the question, "Why then have I been so very wise?" is Solomon's self-appraisal, but in light of his conclusion "Fear God and keep His commandments," we can conclude that he wasn't as wise as he judged himself at this point. After all, he was the one who wrote that "The fear of the LORD is the beginning of wisdom." The Law taught that the fear of the LORD keeps one from sinning (Exodus 20:20) as it did for God's servant Job (Job 1:1). But even though Solomon knew God's Law and its requirements, he chose to disobey it. Thus, his initial conclusion is that everything is meaningless. But we need to remember his ultimate conclusion, "fear God and keep His commandments" (12:13-14).

Another reason that Solomon sounds fatalistic is because "there is no enduring remembrance" for the wise or the fool. Indeed, if there is eternal life, Solomon would have been correct. But in light of Jesus' death and resurrection, we know that death is not the end. "If in Christ we have hope in this life only, we are of all people most to be pitied," is the Apostle Paul's conclusion (1 Cor 15:19). Solomon would have agreed with Mark Twain who said, "The world will

---

12 Fox suggests that verse 13 clarifies that the words "madness and folly" represent a single concept, "foolish madness." Fox, *Ecclesiastes*, 15.

13 The Apostle Paul affirms that death entered the world through sin. See Romans 5.

mourn us for an hour but forget us forever." And yet, Solomon is proven wrong since three thousand years later we read his work that is kept for posterity in the very Word of God, the Bible. Subsequently, godless knowledge combined with discontentment of one's death and remembrance after death leads Solomon to hate life. "So I hated life, because what is done under the sun was grievous to me," he concludes, and that implies that Solomon lacks humility. Solomon is focused solely on himself as he writes, and as he seeks to discover what he can get out of life. His conclusion would have been drastically different if he would have feared God and kept His commandments.

2:18-26 *Godless work leads to lack of vision*

2:18-19 I hated all my toil in which I toil under the sun, seeing that I must leave it to the man who will come after me, and who knows whether he will be wise or a fool? Yet he will be master of all for which I toiled and used my wisdom under the sun. This also is vanity.

Solomon goes from general to specific; first he hates his life, now he hates his work. When God is not the center of one's work, lack of vision renders that work meaningless. Instead of being satisfied to leave behind the fruit of his labors to someone else, he considers this vanity, meaningless, absurd. Would Solomon have been more satisfied if he knew that the one who followed him was wise? His rhetorical question seems to indicate that, but we cannot be certain. In his case, Solomon was succeeded by Rehoboam and Jeroboam I, two kings who did evil in the sight of the LORD (1 Kgs 11-14, 2 Chron 9-13). In God's eyes, they were two fools who did not fear the LORD and who did not obey His commandments. Solomon realizes that it was his wisdom that allowed him to accomplish what he did, but he doesn't seem to give credit to God for that wisdom. After all, Solomon benefited from the leadership of his father David. A son should be grateful to benefit from his father's labor. But, instead of being grateful for God's blessings, Solomon concludes that this is vanity, meaningless, absurd.

2:20-23 So I turned about and gave my heart up to despair
over all the toil of my labors under the sun, because sometimes a
person who has toiled with wisdom and knowledge and skill must
leave everything to be enjoyed by someone who did not toil for it.
This also is vanity and a great evil. What has a man from all the
toil and striving of heart with which he toils beneath the sun? For
all his days are full of sorrow, and his work is a vexation. Even in
the night his heart does not rest. This also is vanity.

While the verb "to turn" could signal a change of heart, it does not happen here. Instead Solomon's feelings of meaninglessness turn to despair.[14] The term "despair" is a little strong in English since the Hebrew could mean "to disillusion oneself,"[15] "to give up for lost,"[16] or "to resign oneself."[17] Longman clarifies that "the Septuagint rendered despair with "to renounce" (apotaxasthai), and so too the Vulgate (renunciavit). The Septuagint opened the way for the faulty view that the repentant Solomon speaks here and renounces his former way of life."[18] He already concluded that leaving your accomplishments behind to someone else was vanity, but now he goes further, affirming that it is a great evil.[19] The rhetorical question posed in verse 22 appears four times in Ecclesiastes (1:3, 2:22, 3:9, and 5:16), and assumes the answer "nothing." What is the rationale for his conclusion? One's days are "full of sorrow, and his work is a vexation." Instead of satisfaction and fulfillment for a work well done, Solomon is full of sorrow. His conclusion is warranted since his view of work is warped by his view of God and His sovereignty. To add insult to

---

14 The Midrash suggests that Solomon actually has a change of heart and realizes that just as he benefits from the work of others, so his work will benefit those who come after him. See Fox, *Ecclesiastes*, 17.

15 Charles F. Whitley, *Koheleth: His Language and Thought* (New York: Walter de Gruyter: 1979), 27.

16 Fox, *Ecclesiastes*, 17.

17 Whybray, *Ecclesiastes*, NCB, 61.

18 Longman, *Ecclesiastes*, 104.

19 The expression "great evil" also occurs in 1 Chronicles 21:17 to refer to David's census taking, in Nehemiah 13:27 to refer to mixed marriages, in Jeremiah 16:10 and 44:7 to refer to God's impending judgment through the Babylonians, and in Hosea 10:15 to refer to Israel's idolatry.

injury, Solomon cannot even enjoy a good night's rest because "his heart does not rest." He anticipates the 20th century proverb "there's no rest for the weary." Leupold summarizes it this way, "The disappointment gnaws at one's heart, and day and night the vexation thought is present. Very properly, then, comes the old refrain that in view of this situation 'this, too, is vanity.'"[20]

> *2:24-25 There is nothing better for a person than that he should eat and drink and find enjoyment in his toil. This also, I saw, is from the hand of God, for apart from him who can eat or who can have enjoyment?*

Solomon is no atheist; he believes in God, and he believes in a God who gives good things. In Solomon's case, to enjoy a good meal is an enjoyment that comes from God. Solomon is not lazy, either. He understands that if he is to eat and drink, he needs to toil. He does understand that "apart from him" one cannot even enjoy eating. So he knows that apart from God one cannot find enjoyment even in the mundaness of daily eating. Solomon believes not just in God, but in His sovereignty. Unfortunately, he does not submit to divine sovereignty. Why is he so blind to see that apart from a correct relationship with God, he cannot find ultimate meaning, satisfaction, or fulfillment? Could it be that his sins put a wall of separation between him and God? Is this not just what God said through the 8th century prophet Isaiah (Isa 59:2), but God made it clear to Solomon that disobedience will result in disappointment and destruction (1 Kgs 9:1-9).

> *26 For to the one who pleases him God has given wisdom and knowledge and joy, but to the sinner he has given the business of gathering and collecting, only to give to one who pleases God. This also is vanity and a striving after wind.*

Is this a half-hearted confession where Solomon sees himself as a sinner? Is he the sinner that God allows to gather and collect "only to give to one who pleases God?" Or, is Solomon the one to whom God gave wisdom, and knowledge, and joy? The Bible clearly states

---

20 Leupold, *Ecclesiastes*, 73.

that God gave Solomon wisdom and knowledge, but at this point, he doesn't seem to have real joy. Solomon apparently is lacking the joy that David experienced when he exclaimed "You have put more joy in my heart than they have when their grain and wine abound" (Ps 4:7), or when he shouted "in your presence there is fullness of joy" (Ps 16:11). Thus, the sinner concludes that even God's sovereign actions amount to "vanity and striving after wind." The concluding refrain then, "Fear God and keep His commandments" (Ecc 12:13) does not apply at this stage of Solomon's life. The imperative is true, but not followed, thus resulting in an unfulfilled life.[21]

Reflections from a psychological perspective

Longings

In this chapter we will examine basic human longings that are left unfulfilled as a result of the fall. Since the fall, man has been attempting to fill a God-shaped void in the human soul, and this is seen through the eyes of Solomon's writing in Ecclesiastes chapter two. The longings of Adam and Eve were readily met prior to the fall. God provided their temporal needs (food, shelter, water, etc), connection and intimacy (with God and with each other) and meaning and purpose (Genesis 3). Often these longings are referred to in Scripture as hunger and thirst (Isaiah 55:1-3). It seems evident that Solomon is clarifying the contrast between the goal of a life pursuing God and the pleasure-seeking goals so commonly seen by mankind. Was Solomon in Ecclesiastes chapter 2 trying to recreate an Eden like experience without the rules ordained by God?

There is a key distinction between goals and desires in chapter 2. A goal is best described as something we have control over, whereas a desire is something we would like but do not have control over. 1 Corinthians 10:31 teaches us that the only correct goal is to glorify God. To set good goals for one's life, it must start with accepting

---

21 Pinker suggests that 2:26 "is a quote that Ecclesiastes rejects, or that it was added by a pious glossator." See Aron Pinker, "How should we understand Ecclesiastes 2:26," in *JBQ* 38.4 (2010), 219-229.

what one can and cannot control. For example, I may want my son to be a good tennis player, but I cannot control his athleticism or his motivation. I can control whether he has a racquet and opportunities to play. The mistake that many of us make is that we try to make our desires (things we cannot control) our goals. I may desire that he become a good tennis player, but it cannot be my goal or else I will be angry if my goal is blocked. I will then be angry at him for blocking my goal, although he has done nothing wrong. An example of a wrong goal of Solomon's was that he hoped that the selfish pursuit of pleasure involving drinking (temporal), women (connection), and work (meaning and purpose) would somehow bring him satisfaction. His selfish desires had become goals apart from God. Is Solomon attempting to use his differing pursuits to satisfy the longings of his heart? Was he ultimately very disappointed that despite his great control as a King, the same fate awaited the wise as did the foolish (Ecc 2:15-17).

Ecclesiastes 2: 1-9:
A long walk on a Hedonic Treadmill will not satisfy.

Solomon was driven by a passion both to know and to understand. However, despite the greatest wisdom given to any man (1 Kings 3:7-14) and his endless pursuits to understand, he found nothing but futility in his searching. Solomon's pursuit of happiness and satisfaction resulted in frustration and disappointment, described in psychology as hedonic adaptation. The concept of hedonic adaptation holds that human beings are born with a "set point" level of overall happiness. Hedonic adaptation further asserts that repeated exposure to painful or pleasurable experiences will only temporarily improve one's level of overall happiness before returning to an individual's "set point." Researchers Solomon and Corbit were able to identify hedonic pathways in the brain that attempt to adapt back to previous levels of happiness.[22] Their research further supports the

---

22 Richard L. Solomon and John D. Corbit, "An Opponent-Process Theory of Motivation: II. Cigarette Addiction," *Journal of Abnormal Psychology 81*, no. 2 (1973): 158-71

notion of hedonic adaptation by showing biological adaptation in the brain. For example, if a man receives an inheritance of an ocean front property from a distant, unknown relative, the beautiful home will only temporarily improve his happiness before he returns to his previous level of happiness. In essence, circumstances and temporary pleasures do not bring us happiness. The inherent problem is that all the deeds or effort expended to acquire material possessions will inevitably not deliver the hoped for reward, and thus humans are left feeling disappointment.

A British psychologist named Michael Eysenck was the first to coin the term "Hedonic Treadmill."[23] The idea of the Hedonic Treadmill insinuates that the pursuit of happiness will result in a person's continuing to walk but failing to get anywhere. The Hedonic Treadmill appears to consistently show evidence of people's frustration with their toil and success, whether it has to do with wealth, possessions, health, or even physical attractiveness.[24] Solomon demonstrates the

---

23 Martin E. P. Seligman, *Authentic Happiness: Using the New Positive Psychology to Realize Your Potential for Lasting Fulfillment.* (New York: Free Press, 2004), 50-55."source":"Open WorldCat","event-place":"New York","abstract":"Publisher description: Positive Psychology focuses on strengths rather than weaknesses, asserting that happiness is not the result of good genes or luck. Seligman teaches readers that happiness can be cultivated by identifying and using many of the strengths and traits that they already possess -- including kindness, originality, humor, optimism, and generosity. By frequently calling upon their \"signature strengths\" in all the crucial realms of life, readers will not only develop natural buffers against misfortune and the experience of negative emotion, they will move their lives up to a new, more positive plane. Drawing on groundbreaking psychological research, Seligman shows how Positive Psychology is shifting the profession's paradigm away from its narrow-minded focus on pathology, victimology, and mental illness to positive emotion, virtue and strength, and positive institutions. Seligman provides the Signature Strengths Survey along with a variety of brief tests that can be used to measure how much positive emotion readers experience, in order to help determine what their highest strengths are.","ISBN":"0743222989 9780743222983","shortTitle":"Authentic happiness","language":"English","author":[{"family":"Seligman","given":"Martin E. P"}],"issued":{"date-parts":[["2004"]]}}}],"schema":"https://github.com/citation-style-language/schema/raw/master/csl-citation.json"}

24 Ibid., 49."source":"Open WorldCat","event-place":"New York","abstract":"Publisher description: Positive Psychology focuses on strengths rather than weaknesses, asserting that happiness is not the result of good genes or luck. Seligman teaches readers that happiness can be cultivated by identifying and using many of the

principle of hedonic adaptation in these verses (1-14). He discovers that endless pursuits of pleasure leave us no happier or fulfilled and that the pointless walk on the hedonic treadmill is even biologically created to stop us from experiencing any lasting peace or happiness that we seek. Solomon then shows us the psychological consequences of this prideful and self-gratifying pursuit. (2:17).

It seems that Solomon thinks that if we were to look at his underlying belief, he would appear to believe that for his toil, he is justified to receive a reward for his efforts (2:10-11). This belief is faulty because it is inherently selfish. In fact, if someone is rewarded for his effort, he will likely be frustrated or angry because "reward-based" motivations will not bring satisfaction and will ultimately lead toward vexation and disappointment. In verses nine and ten, we begin to get a glimpse of the thoughts and actions that pervade Solomon's life. Solomon's thoughts appear to be dominated by his great accomplishments and that he has become greater than others before him. Throughout the entire book Solomon repeatedly recounts all the ways that he has surpassed his predecessors, but he fails to even mention how the Lord has blessed him in his accomplishments. As one looks throughout chapter 2, it is difficult to ignore the number of times that Solomon uses the word "I." Did the wisest man on earth lose his humility that was so evident when God first granted him his wisdom (1 Kings 3:7-14)?

---

strengths and traits that they already possess -- including kindness, originality, humor, optimism, and generosity. By frequently calling upon their \"signature strengths\" in all the crucial realms of life, readers will not only develop natural buffers against misfortune and the experience of negative emotion, they will move their lives up to a new, more positive plane. Drawing on groundbreaking psychological research, Seligman shows how Positive Psychology is shifting the profession's paradigm away from its narrow-minded focus on pathology, victimology, and mental illness to positive emotion, virtue and strength, and positive institutions. Seligman provides the Signature Strengths Survey along with a variety of brief tests that can be used to measure how much positive emotion readers experience, in order to help determine what their highest strengths are.","ISBN":"0743222989 9780743222983","shortTitle":"Authentic happiness","language":"English","author":[{"family":"Seligman","given":"Martin E. P"}],"issued":{"date-parts":[["2004"]]}},"locator":"49"}],"schema":"https://github.com/citation-style-language/schema/raw/master/csl-citation.json"}

Godless pursuits vs. true meaning and purpose

There is often a clash in the lives of people when they realize that sinful, selfish goals produce harmful consequences (2:18-22). Essentially, as sinful and broken people, we often have mistaken goals which result in despair and grief. We experience this grief because our hope was placed in earthly pleasures (2:23) that are attempting to fulfill a God-shaped void. The truth from a psychological perspective is that nothing on earth, whether it is pride, wealth, or lust of the flesh, will completely satisfy our souls, because God is the true source of meaning and purpose. This is a hard truth to accept for many people as it was for Solomon (2:23). A change in perspective requires reverent humility, accepting both our small role in God's design and the fact that this world cannot satisfy us. The acceptance of this truth allows believers to see they have all that they need in God. Once their perspective changes to understand that they have what they need in Him, they are free to enjoy God's gifts. They are also free to love and care for others without trying to control or manipulate them to meet their own mistaken goals.

Ecclesiastes 3

3:1-8
A timeless poem

3:9-15
He made everything beautiful in its time

3:16-22
From dust to dust

3:1-8 A timeless poem

The first part of chapter 3 is a poem in which Solomon, like a masterful artisan, intertwines optimistic and pessimistic themes. The poem is arranged in chiastic form,[1] and after the introductory assertion in verse 1, verses 2-8 are made up of fourteen antitheses.[2] Krüger suggests that the "28 (4 x 7) 'matters' in 14 (2 x 7) pairs...could indicate that here 'seven, the number of perfection' is supposed to be developed into 'four, the cardinal points of the heavens,' in order that 'the fullness of the time at human's disposal' can be described as ordered cosmos."[3]

---

1 Bartholomew, *Ecclesiastes*, 161. A chiasm is a literary device where a sequence of components are repeated in reverse order. The name comes from the Greek letter chi.

2 Murphy, *Ecc'esiastes*, 32.

3 Krüger, *Qoheleth*, 76.

3:1 For everything there is a season,
and a time for every matter under heaven.[4]

As he analyzes how things are under the sun, Solomon does not make a moral pronouncement or a theological statement;[5] he simply makes an observation. The following pairs are descriptive, not prescriptive.[6] He is not saying that one should kill or hate, but as he has observed fallen humanity, he saw that sometimes people are born, and sometimes they die, sometimes they laugh and sometimes they cry, sometimes they love, and unfortunately, sometimes they hate. Tamez suggests that the redeeming qualities of this passage can come only from the understanding that the affirmation "for everything there is a season" is a utopian phrase that orders real life in the midst of slavish toil."[7]

3:2 a time to be born, and a time to die; a time to plant,
and a time to pluck up what is planted;

Life and death are generally outside of human control. The infinitive "to be born/to give birth" appears only three times in the Old Testament (Gen 4:2; 25:24; Isa 26:17), which most scholars translate passively as "to be born." Since the verb is passive in form in 7:2, the vast majority of versions translate it in the passive voice as well.

The second set of concepts arranged in antithetical fashion is presented also with two infinitive constructs, "to plant," and "to pluck up." The verb "to plant" parallels well "to give birth," as "both

---

4 For the structure of verse 1 see Tod Linafelt and F.W. Dobbs-Allsopp, "Poetic Line Structure in Qoheleth 3:1," in VT 60 (2010):249-259. Blenkinsopp wrongly suggests that 3:2-8 is "cited but not authored by Qoheleth," who later "added a title and a brief commentary." See Joseph Blenkinsopp, "Ecclesiastes 3:1-15: Another Interpretation," in *JSOT* 66 (1995):55-64. On the other hand, Stohlmann states that "this poem is an expression of faith of an Old Testament saint. He believes all time, every fixed and appointed time in man's lifetime, is in God's hands." See Stephen C. Stohlmann, "Everything Beautiful in its Time: A Meditation on Ecclesiastes or The Preacher 3:1-15," in Concordia Journal 7 (1981):178-181.

5 Garrett, *Proverbs, Ecclesiastes, Song of Songs*, 298.

6 Longman, *Ecclesiastes*, 114.

7 Elsa Tamez, "Ecclesiastes: A Reading from the Periphery," in *Interpretation* 55/3 (2001): 250.

are ways of giving life."[8] Just as one plucks up a plant, one's life can end abruptly, or one can just wither away.

3:3 a time to kill, and a time to heal;
a time to break down, and a time to build up;

Solomon is not saying that one should kill, and he doesn't address "ethical questions of what constitutes just war;"[9] rather, as he observed life under the sun, he saw that sometimes people are killed. The negative "to kill" is contrasted with the positive "to heal." Longman asserts that even though these verbs are not "exact semantic opposites," the first can be regarded as the intentional taking of one's life, while the second can refer "to efforts to preserve life."[10] The second pair of breaking down/building up generally evokes the imagery of a tent or dwelling being torn town and built up. All these point to the end and beginning of an endeavor.

3:4 a time to weep, and a time to laugh;
a time of mourning, and of dancing;

Because humans are emotional beings, broken covenants, promises, and hearts lead people living their lives under the sun to weep. On the other hand, people whose hearts are merry laugh. The Apostle Paul encourages us to "rejoice with those who rejoice, and weep with those who weep" (Rom 12:15). As the shadow of death descends upon the lives of mortals, mourning becomes part of life. The verb "to mourn" "is specifically the bewailing of the dead at a funeral."[11] On the other hand, at times, those who rejoice break into dancing.[12]

The placement of the weep/mourn pair after kill/pluck up is not accidental because weeping and mourning come naturally after life is taken away. The same can be said about the laugh/dance pair following a time to heal and a time to build up. Laughter follows healing

---

8 Garrett, *Proverbs, Ecclesiastes, Song of Songs,* 298.

9 Ibid.

10 Longman, *Ecclesiastes,* 115.

11 Michael V. Fox, *Ecclesiastes,* 21.

12 1 Sam 18:6, 2 Sam 6:14, Psalm 30:11, 150:4, Jeremiah 31:13.

just like dancing is a great way to celebrate the successful completion of a building.

3:5 a time to cast away stones, and a time to gather stones together; a time to embrace, and a time to refrain from embracing;

In a predominately agrarian society, the casting away of stones can be thought of in the context of clearing a field for cultivation, while the gathering of stones can be thought of in the context of building a wall. The casting of stones could also have a military nuance if these stones are meant to ruin an enemy's field by throwing stones into it (2 Kgs 3:19, 25). If this is the case, the pair fails to fit with the embracing motif in the second pair of infinitives. Thus, some scholars prefer to read the casting and gathering of stones as a euphemism for sexual intercourse. Robert Gordis quotes the Midrash: "A time to cast stones—when your wife is clean (menstrually), and a time to gather stones in—when your wife is unclean."[13]

The second pair of opposites is not presented as opposites but rather with the positive "to embrace," and the self-controlling "to refrain from embracing." The verb "to embrace" can be used for a simple hug given to relatives (Gen 29:13, 2 Kgs 4:16), and it can also refer to sexual intercourse (Prov 5:20, Song 8:3). While a sexual connotation might fit better with the first set of opposites, we can leave the meaning as ambiguous, as the writer did, instead of forcing the text and its interpretation.

3:6 a time to seek, and a time to lose; a time to keep, and a time to cast away;

It is difficult to interpret this verse without having an exact social setting. If Solomon was thinking about a household setting, then this could refer to something sought and found since the antonym of "to seek" is not "to lose." In the same setting, one can keep what he/she has accumulated over time, but at some point, parting with such re-

---

13 Quoted in Longman, 116. Longman is not convinced of this view but agrees with Whybray's more literal approach, suggesting that the clearing the field of stones prepares it for its agricultural use. See Longman, *Ecclesiastes*, 116.

sources might be wise. Longman asserts that "just as it is impossible for people to know the day of their death, control their weeping and laughing or their mourning and rejoicing, so it is hard, sometimes impossible, to know when something is irrevocably lost."[14] Perhaps, the ambiguous reference to the object of the search helps us to see that Solomon makes a general, rather than a particular statement.[15]

> *3:7 a time to tear, and a time to sew;*
> *a time to keep silence, and a time to speak;*

The context of the first pair can be domestic or related to mourning. If it is domestic, it speaks of the normal wear and tear of clothes that, after tearing, are sewn. However, when looking at the parallel "to keep silence," the pair could refer to the tearing of clothes as a sign of mourning. The mourning pain can render one speechless, and silence is often the companion of one who suffers. The motif of proper timing in speech is a common theme within wisdom literature and could indicate any number of situations.[16]

> *3:8 a time to love, and a time to hate;*
> *a time for war, and a time for peace.*

The chiastic structure of verse 8 is different from any other of the set of pairs in the poem.[17]

14 Longman, *Ecclesiastes*, 117.
15 Ibid.
16 Prov 10:19, 13:3, 15:23, 16:24, 17:27, 21:23, 25:11. See Longman, *Ecclesiastes*, 117.
17 Longman, *Ecclesiastes*, 118.

The difference between the pairs is not just structural but also semantic in that while love and hate are well within the range of the individual, war and peace are events that involve communities of people. Although this could illustrate how the timing of an individual's actions can relate to the actions of the broader community, Solomon is not advocating them; rather, he "describes them as parts of the full spectrum of human experience."[18] Tamez hopes that we would not allow ourselves to "become dehumanized in a dehumanizing society."[19] She sees the proverbial silver lining on the horizon and encourages the ones living under the sun to "know that better times will come because everything has its time and season."[20]

The poem deals with a wide range of issues such as time, life and death, love and war, humanity and deity. Solomon's quest leads him close to despair, but from the edge of the abyss he correctly concludes that one must fear God. Even so, one must not view lightly the complexities of time and human endeavors. Life does not come with easy answers but tough questions which may or may not find answers "under the sun." Qoheleth's message is the same today for the whole globe as it was for the people of the ancient Near East: Recognize your humanity, embrace the mysteries of life, and fear the Creator God.

3:9-15 He made everything beautiful in its time

> *3:9-11 What gain has the worker from his toil? I have seen the business that God has given to the children of man to be busy with. He has made everything beautiful in its time. Also, he has put eternity into man's heart, yet so that he cannot find out what God has done from the beginning to the end.*

The rhetorical question "what gain has the worker from his toil?" anticipates the answer "Nothing." Indeed, apart from a correct relationship with God, one does not experience even the satisfaction of

---

18 Ibid.
19 Tamez, "Ecclesiastes: A reading from the periphery," 259.
20 Ibid.

work well done. Verse 10 actually points to the fact that God afflicts people with work. Garrett correctly points out that "work is not simply a part of nature but is an affliction from God (Gen 3:17-19)."[21] Even so, Solomon recognizes that God makes everything beautiful[22] in its time. "Everything" can refer to the pairs found in verses 1-8. Moreover, God put eternity in the human heart.[23] The idea of eternity is not a human invention. Rather, God places the idea of eternity in one's heart to understand that life is more than what is on this side of the grave. In fact, life after death in the presence of God is the best since it's absent of tears, pain, and death.[24]

> *3:12-14 I perceived that there is nothing better for them than to be joyful and to do good as long as they live; also that everyone should eat and drink and take pleasure in all his toil-- this is God's gift to man. I perceived that whatever God does endures forever; nothing can be added to it, nor anything taken from it. God has done it, so that people fear before him.*

Solomon's quest has left him empty and unfulfilled. Yet, in his desperation, he cries out "Carpe Diem!" Seize the day! Some fulfillment will come from enjoying life, and some fulfillment will come from doing good. Indeed, doing good is not a new concept in the Old Testament. Through the Law of Moses, God instructed His people to feed the poor and take care of the sojourner in the land.[25]

Solomon's theology is orthodox. He knows that "whatever God does endures forever." Therefore, humanity's response to who God is and what He has done should be fear. The fear of the LORD is a very

---

21 Garrett, *Proverbs, Ecclesiastes, Song of Songs,* 299.

22 The word can also be translated "appropriate."

23 Some amend the word 'lm (eternity) into 'ml (toil) changing the verse to "He also placed toil in their hearts." See Fox, *Ecclesiastes,* 23, and Brian P. Gault, "A Reexamination of 'Eternity' in Ecclesiastes 3:11," in *Bibliotheca Sacra* 165 (2008):39-57.

24 "He will wipe away every tear from their eyes, and death shall be no more, neither shall there be mourning, nor crying, nor pain anymore, for the former things have passed away" (Rev 21:4).

25 Exod 23:11, Lev 19:10, Deut 24:19.

important concept in wisdom literature and it does not refer to a paralyzing fear, but a fear that makes us be in awe of God, a fear that makes us run away from evil, and a fear that draws us close to Him.[26]

> *3:15 That which is, already has been; that which is to be, already has been; and God seeks what has been driven away.*

Verse 15 echoes the thought of 1:9 "What has been is what will be, and what has been done is what will be done, and there is nothing new under the sun." The new thought that "God seeks what has been driven away," refers to the fact that God's search is for the purpose of caring. Thus, God looks after the poor and the oppressed.[27]

3:16-22 From dust to dust

> *3:16-17 Moreover, I saw under the sun that in the place of justice, even there was wickedness, and in the place of righteousness, even there was wickedness. I said in my heart, God will judge the righteous and the wicked, for there is a time for every matter and for every work.*

In a godless society, wickedness reigns supreme, while in a godly society justice rules. Solomon observes that under the sun (on earth) the judicial system is corrupt. He does not address the methods of corruption, nor its details, but just affirms its existence. Solomon returns to his "there is a time for everything" premise, showing confidence that God will make all things right when He will judge the righteous and the wicked. Indeed, the idea that Yahweh is the ultimate Judge, rewarding the righteous and punishing the wicked is a consistent theme throughout Scripture.[28]

> *3:18-21 I said in my heart with regard to the children of man that God is testing them that they may see that they themselves are but*

---

26 Job 28:28 Psalm 111:10, Prov 1:7, 8:13, 9:10.

27 "Sforno says this means that God will seek out – and restore – the persecuted of Israel. See Fox, *Ecclesiastes*, 25.

28 Isa 2:4, Jer 11:20, Ezek 7:3, 33:20, Acts 10:42, 2 Tim 4:1, Heb 12:23, 1 Peter 1:17, Rev 19:11, 20:12-13.

beasts. For what happens to the children of man and what happens
to the beasts is the same; as one dies, so dies the other. They all have
the same breath, and man has no advantage over the beasts, for all
is vanity. All go to one place. All are from the dust, and to dust all
return. Who knows whether the spirit of man goes upward and the
spirit of the beast goes down into the earth?

Solomon's view of the afterlife is warped since he concludes that
death brings both humans and animals to an expected end. The view
that humans are no different from the animals goes against his father's Spirit-filled words, "What is man that you are mindful of him,
and the son of man that you care for him? Yet, you have made him
a little lower than the heavenly beings and crowed him with glory
and honor" (Psalm 8:4-5). It is true that both humans and animals
have a body (flesh) and the breath of life, but they do not share the
same afterlife. Because of his warped view about life and the afterlife,
Solomon concludes that all is vanity, everything is meaningless. The
question, "Who knows whether the spirit of man goes upward and
the spirit of the beast goes down into earth?" seems to demand the
answer, "No one knows!" While Solomon might not deny there is an
afterlife, he definitely does not project certainty.

3:22 So I saw that there is nothing better than that a man
should rejoice in his work, for that is his lot.
Who can bring him to see what will be after him?

Since there is uncertainty when it comes to his view of the afterlife, Solomon encourages humans to rejoice in their present work.
This is not a new development for Solomon since he argued for such
carpe-diem philosophy earlier in the book (2:24-26, 3:12-14). A
view such as this is not only fatalistic, but lacks vision. Although
man cannot see what will happen after he dies, he must trust in the
sovereignty of the Creator God who is control.

Thinking about the rest of Scripture, we are reminded that Jesus
died to redeem us from the meaninglessness Solomon experienced.
Today's Christian cannot live with the warped and incomplete view
of the afterlife that Solomon had. Rather, we take comfort in the

fact that Christ-followers will spend an eternity in the presence of the Lord. Those who reject Jesus' death and resurrection will spend a Godless eternity in hell.

Reflections from a psychological perspective

Human choice as it pertains to time and perspective

Solomon reiterates in these verses that God is in control of the world and that death is inevitable for all. In the movie *National Treasure*, the main character attempts to solve the riddle, "What is the debt that all men must pay?" and of course the answer is death.29 There is no greater proof of our inability to control fate in this world than the fact that we will all die. If I could control my mortality, I would, but I cannot. It is clearly stated in Genesis 3:19, "By the sweat of your face you shall eat bread, till you return to the ground, for out of it you were taken; for you are dust, and to dust you shall return." So if we are all destined to die and if we have very limited control, then what should we do with this reality? Do we fight God for control of something that we cannot control? Or do we accept God's sovereignty and choose to fear God?

Solomon also appears to be emphasizing that order in the world is illusive and it is not within mankind's finite mind to understand God's timeline for events (Figure 1:A-D). As Barrick states, "This text challenges unbelievers, because people without a relationship with God seek to be gods themselves. Unregenerate mankind engages in a crusade to control time in order to gain an escape from individual responsibility and to obtain what they think will provide peace and security."30 Many people will get stuck in this cycle as they are unable to assign meaning and understanding to the painful events they have experienced. As a result they continue to seek personal answers or choose skepticism about life. Accepting one's limitations and the unpredictability of life is a terrifying ordeal. These passages in Eccle-

---

29 Jon Turteltaub, *National Treasure*, Buena Vista Home Entertainment, 2005.
30 William D. Barrick, *Ecclesiastes*, 62.

siastes do not appear to indicate that life is totally out of control. Instead, I hear a plea to be reflective and to accept the truth that God is sovereign. The famous quote from Socrates states, "An unexamined life is not worth living."[31] As Socrates emphasized self-examination, so Solomon encourages his readers to become reflective and attentive to what season of life they are in. A contemplative, reflective person will not dwell on the details and troubles of life, but will instead choose to focus on the Creator of the universe.

Solomon also seems to be saying we are responsible for our choices that occur within God's timeline (Figure 1: D-F). Noted psychiatrist William Glasser developed his own theory of counseling called Choice Theory.[32] Glasser's theory maintains that the only person's behavior (thoughts and actions) that we can control is our own. Glasser further asserts that attempts to control others frequently results in frustration and destruction of close relationships. Solomon seems to be indicating that in times of pain we are to respond in Godly ways. Solomon does not seem to be sending a hedonistic message to pursue pleasure amidst these passages. Instead, he seems to be saying that it is our job to accept what we can and can't control. Can we accept the fact that both pain and pleasure will come throughout our lives? Or do we choose to blindly maneuver in our world, looking for something new to satisfy our souls? The emptiness that we feel in our souls cannot be satisfied (Ecc 3:11) this side of heaven, and the God-shaped void in our souls will not be satisfied with Satan's distractions (Ecc 2:1-11).

A tension often exists between our finite ability and God's sovereignty. We must choose to rest in the knowledge that His ways are far superior to our ways. Even though we cannot comprehend God's order in time, it is still our responsibility to try to determine whether it is a time to "do good" (Ecc 3:12). There is a time for everything (Ecc 3:1-8) whether it be peace or war, mourning or dance. How then should we conduct ourselves in this time? The reader is left

---

31 Thomas C. Brickhouse and Nicholas D. Smith, *Plato's Socrates* (Oxford: OUP, 1994), 201.

32 William Glasser, *Choice Theory: A New Psychology of Personal Freedom* (New York: Harper Perennial, 1999), 16.

with the truth that despite our very limited ability to grasp God's timeline, we must accept responsibility for our lack of control and choose to "do good" (obey God) in our time (Figure 2: A-F). Following God involves humility, fearing Him (Prov. 1:7) and obeying His commands. In so doing, we can experience the freedom to trust in God's goodness and thus experience joy in all of our toil. Therefore, there is nothing better for us then to fear God throughout our lives, to pursue His ways, and to also enjoy the rich gifts of God.

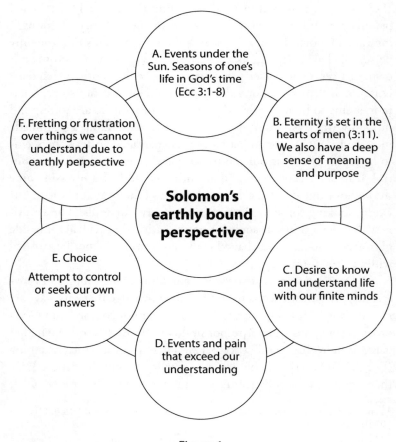

Figure 1

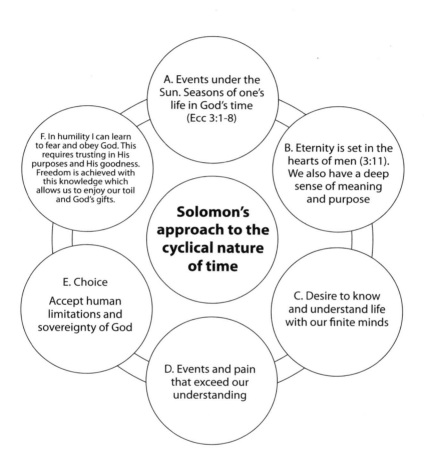

Figure 2

Ecclesiastes 4

4:1-3
The tears of the oppressed

4:4-8
The meaninglessness of work

4:9-12
The value of companionship

4:13-16
A wise child better than a foolish king

4:1-3 The tears of the oppressed

Again I saw all the oppressions that are done under the sun.
And behold, the tears of the oppressed1, and they had no one to
comfort them! On the side of their oppressors there was power,
and there was no one to comfort them. And I thought the dead
who are already dead more fortunate than the living who are
still alive. But better than both is he who has not yet been and
has not seen the evil deeds that are done under the sun.

As Solomon observes what is happening on the earth, he sees the
tears of the oppressed. In contrast with the power of oppressors, Solomon paints a portrait of the oppressed who have no comforter.[2]

---

1 For a suggested emendation from "oppressed" to "punished" see Aron Pinker,
"The Oppressed in Qohelet 4:1," in *VT* 61.3 (2011):393-405.

2 Fink suggests that this is "about the exploitation, by wealthier classes, of the people settled on the land and of the hard workers living in cities." See Norbert Fink,
Qoheleth: A Continental Commentary (Minneapolis, MN: Fortress, 2003), 68.

Solomon identifies two issues here: the oppressed are treated with injustice and the oppressed lack a human or divine comforter. While Solomon doesn't ask for the cessation of injustice, he seems to be inviting the reader to share in his sorrow. Not too surprising, Solomon concludes that the dead are better off than those who are alive. It seems that for him death is the ultimate resolver of issues. Furthermore, the unborn is better yet since he/she has not yet experienced the injustices of the living.[3]

This passage is yet another reason why Christians need to read Ecclesiastes Christologically. Solomon's perspective cannot be the perspective of the redeemed who have experienced Christ's salvation. Even though we experience injustice,[4] we look to the Righteous Judge who will ultimately punish all evil and injustice.

Reflections from a psychological perspective

This fourth chapter of Ecclesiastes appears to have many similarities with the thoughts of one of the most overshadowed pioneers in the field of psychology, Alfred Adler (1870-1937). His theories about human nature were radically different from that of the far more famous and deterministic Sigmund Freud. Early in his career Adler served as one of the first four members of Sigmund Freud's Psychoanalytic Society and actually served as the president before a major split became apparent in 1911 (11:8-11). Alfred Adler, who became a Protestant in 1904, spent the rest of his life developing his own theory called Individual Psychology. Adler developed a more holistic and socially oriented approach. He believed in the uniqueness and creativity of each individual to develop a style of life and that, within this lifestyle, each person has both the freedom of choice and personal responsibility for his or her actions. Individual Psychology maintains that all human beings are goal-directed and that they move purposefully towards goals

---

3 This verse has similar nuances to Job 3:3-5 and Jeremiah 20:18. For the interplay of death and possessions see Matthew S. Rindge, "Mortality and Enjoyment: The Interplay of Death and Possessions in Qoheleth," in *CBQ* 73.2 (2011):265-280.

4 As I write, ISIS, an extremist Islamic group, is persecuting and killing Christians in the Middle East.

that attract them. However, these goals that individuals choose may or may not be useful for the individual or mankind. It is the individual's goals that drive human behavior.

Adlerians believe that many of our goals are set in middle childhood through the modeling of our parents and our social system. The faulty belief or private logic that one must continually seek power to avoid feeling weak around others is one example. Consequently, this faulty private logic will produce problems in a person's character and his relationships with others, when he chooses to oppress them to avoid feeling vulnerable.[5] Furthermore, Adlerians believe that the individual can change this private logic to a more ideal goal which Adler referred to as the "pursuit of perfection." Many Adlerians see this perfection evidenced in the life of Christ and that the pursuit of this perfection or Christ-like behaviors is in line with this theoretical orientation.

> To strive towards God, to be in Him, to follow His call, to be one with Him-from this goal of striving, there follow attitude, thinking and feeling....Man as an ever-striving being could not be like God. God, who is eternally complete, who directs the stars, who is the master of fates, who elevates man from his lowliness to Himself, who speaks from the cosmos to every single human soul.[6]

Therefore, if an individual who believes that the pursuit of power will satisfy his longing for power, it then becomes the role of the Adlerian Christian counselor to address this behavior in light of the ideal goal which is to be Christ-like. Solomon appears to be making an observation of mankind's useless behaviors around power. He saw the injustice that is done by pursuing faulty goals of seeking power over fellow man and the subsequent oppression of others (Ecc 5:8). Alfred Adler's view was that the pursuit of power and injustice is a faulty goal to overcome man's sense of inferiority (awareness of

---

5 Guy J. Manaster and Raymond J. Corsini, *Individual Psychology: Theory and Practice* (Itasca, Ill: F.E. Peacock, 1982), 30-31.

6 Alfred Adler, Heinz Ludwig Ansbacher, and Rowena R. Ansbacher, *Superiority and Social Interest: A Collection of Later Writings,* 3rd revised edition, (New York: Norton, 1979), 275.

his lowliness) by overcompensating and oppressing others to escape one's own feelings of inferiority.

Solomon repeatedly makes reference in Ecclesiastes to the futility of life. He even goes as far as to say it is better not to have been born (4:2). It appears that Solomon is raising an existential question regarding whether a life pursuing goals of power and superiority is a life wasted. Some Adlerians view the existential question of meaning and purpose as a fundamental question that all mankind must answer. Some have difficulty embracing the fact that death is unavoidable and that neither you nor I can alter that fact. It is crucial for all of us to embrace the fact that we are ultimately answerable to God. When we accept that fact, it frees us to pursue a life in reality that embraces both our meaning and purpose.

Solomon appears to be pointing out that in the pursuit of meaning, seeking power and the oppression of others is a dead end road. It is only when we view Solomon's statements Christologically that we can see meaning in Christ's suffering, crucifixion, and resurrection. Only in the life and work of Christ will we find both the goal of perfection we have sought and the meaning, purpose, and hope which His resurrection provides to guide our lives.

4:4-8 The meaninglessness of wrong-motivated work

> *4:4-8 Then I saw that all toil and all skill in work come from a man's envy of his neighbor. This also is vanity and a striving after wind. The fool folds his hands and eats his own flesh. Better is a handful of quietness than two hands full of toil and a striving after wind. Again, I saw vanity under the sun: one person who has no other, either son or brother, yet there is no end to all his toil, and his eyes are never satisfied with riches, so that he never asks, "For whom am I toiling and depriving myself of pleasure?" This also is vanity and an unhappy business.*[7]

---

7 Wazana suggests that 4:4-8 makes some allusions to the evil eye concept –"the belief that spiteful looks can damage one's health, fertility, or property." See Nili

Wrongly motivated work leads to emptiness. If one's toil—even skilled work—is motivated by envy, then it will lead only to a sense of meaninglessness. But the one who works out of envy is not deemed a fool by Solomon; rather, the lazy one is. The hyperbole paints the picture of a lazy person[8] who is so slothful that he resorts to eating his own flesh rather than getting up to work for his food. (Or . . . eating his own flesh rather than working ...)

Verse 6 reiterates the idea of Proverbs 15:16, "Better is a little with the fear of the LORD than great treasure and trouble with it." Verse 7 advances the idea of this teaching. A hard worker without a proper balance of work and rest and whose money is his only kin[9] will be disappointed in the end. Not only will all things prove meaningless, but in the process, he will forego other pleasures. Solomon concludes that this is meaningless and an unhappy business.[10]

Can a redeemed follower of Christ live with such a viewpoint? Certainly not! Our call is to "work heartily, as for the Lord and not for men."[11]

Reflections from a psychological perspective

Solomon appears to be revisiting the purpose of the motives behind our labor. Are we laboring with the goal of glorifying God? Or are we laboring to bring glory, honor, and riches to ourselves? Solomon is not telling us to quit working but instead to quit overworking, because striving motivated by a sense of entitlement produces envy and jealousy. This in turn will lead only to meaninglessness. Adlerians utilize the term "Fictional Finalism" which suggests that humans in their freedom of choice develop personal private goals. Individuals are not necessarily aware of these goals because some of them are

Wazana, "A Case of the Evil Eye: Qohelet 4:4-8," in *JBL* 126, 4 (2007):685-702.

8 Longman, *Ecclesiastes,* 138.

9 Garrett, *Proverbs, Ecclesiastes, Song of Songs,* 307.

10 The literal Hebrew translation of the last three words in verse 8 is "it is an evil task."

11 Colossians 3:23.

set in childhood. However, we will experience emotions and behave consistently with these personal private goals, which lead us to a fictitious end result[12] (12:14-15). In essence, we make goals that are fiction (for example: being motivated by jealousy/envy coming from a sense of entitlement) and then seek to live them out in reality. Consequently, we can expect this envy and jealousy to produce dangerous emotions and behaviors. We see this in Proverbs 6:34, "For jealousy makes a man furious, and he will not spare when he takes revenge." It is from the faulty belief in a sense of entitlement that produces envious desires and coveting as James describes in James 3:14-16: "But if you have bitter jealousy and selfish ambition in your hearts, do not boast and be false to the truth. This is not the wisdom that comes down from above, but is earthly, unspiritual, demonic. For where jealousy and selfish ambition exist, there will be disorder and every vile practice." The goal of Christian counselors is to help clients pursue goals and beliefs that will lead to glorifying God as well as providing meaningful, God-honoring interactions with those around us.

Solomon is warning all of us against another faulty belief he observed in his life and in others. Solomon, whose wealth was unmatched in all of Israel, knew that striving after labor and riches was a fictional goal. "Then I considered all that my hands had done and the toil I had expended in doing it, and behold, all was vanity and a striving after wind, and there was nothing to be gained under the sun" (Ecc 2:11). This pursuit only produces vexation and isolation. God wants us to pursue the balance illustrated in verse 6. We must pursue our labor for the right motives and with the purpose of glorifying God with our work. This is illustrated by Paul in 1 Corinthians 10:3: "So, whether you eat or drink, or whatever you do, do all to the glory of God."

---

12 Guy J. Manaster and Raymond J. Corsini, *Individual Psychology: Theory and Practice*, 14-15.

4:9-12 *The value of companionship*

Two are better than one, because they have a good reward for their toil. For if they fall, one will lift up his fellow. But woe to him who is alone when he falls and has not another to lift him up! Again, if two lie together, they keep warm, but how can one keep warm alone? And though a man might prevail against one who is alone, two will withstand him- a threefold cord is not quickly broken.

From very pragmatic points of view, companionship is better than isolationism. From a business perspective, companionship is better because it produces a larger profit (v. 9). From a practical/personal perspective, companionship is better because people can help each other in time of need (v. 10).[13] The lying together here is to be taken into its plain sense, not a sexual one. Garrett is correct when he points out that the image is "derived from that of travelers who must lie beside each other to stay warm on cold desert nights."[14] When one is confronted by an enemy, two is better than one, but three is best. Ogden is right when he asserts that "Qoheleth suggests that to live life under the sun with a companion who will share its possible burdens is the wisest and most reasonable course of action."[15] Some suggest that the author may be referring to a well- known ancient Near Eastern proverb. Some early church fathers tried to tie this passage to a lot of ideas, such as the Trinity, and calling the three cords faith, hope, and love. Some have even seen Christ as the "friend" or "companion."[16] While these concepts are orthodox when one devel-

---

13 Dahood suggests that "Qoheleth composed his work employing Phoenician or defective orthography" that originally read, "For it the one falls, His companion will lift him up." See Mitchell Joseph Dahood. "Scriptio Defectiva in Qoheleth 4:10a," in *Biblica* 49.2 (1968): 243.

14 Garrett, *Proverbs, Ecclesiastes, Song of Songs,* 308. Garrett stretches this to suggest that "the usage is here metaphorical for emotional comfort against the coldness of the world."

15 Graham S. Ogden, "The Mathematics of Wisdom: Qoheleth 4:1-12," in *VT* 34.4 (1984): 446-453.

16 Longman, *Ecclesiastes,* 142-144. Or is the author using irony here? See Sophie Ramond, Ý a-t-il de l'ironie dans le livre de Qohélet?" in *VT* 60 (2010):621-640.

ops a biblical theology after searching both the Old and the New Testaments, they cannot be derived from this passage alone.

Reflections from a psychological perspective

This passage is consistent with the last thirty years of psychological research on human connection. The research suggests that both your physical and mental health are worsened by poor social connectedness[17]. Psychological research clearly supports Solomon's observations that human beings were designed to be in relationship with one another. Human connectedness serves as a buffer against stress and produces preventive responses for both mental health and health related conditions. In fact, social isolation has repeatedly been identified as the single best predictor of someone's developing a mental health diagnosis.

4:13-16 A wise child better than a foolish king

> *Better was a poor and wise youth than an old and foolish king who no longer knew how to take advice. For he went from prison to the throne, though in his own kingdom he had been born poor. I saw all the living who move about under the sun, along with that youth who was to stand in the king's place. There was no end of all the people, all of whom he led. Yet those who come later will not rejoice in him. Surely this also is vanity and a striving after wind.[18]*

Solomon knows that gray hair does not translate into wisdom. It seems that he is not writing hypothetically, but rather that he is writing about certain historical characters.[19] Either way, the conclu-

---

17 P. A. Thoitis, "Mechanisms Linking Social Ties and Support to Physical and Mental Health," *Journal of health and Social Behavior* 52, no. 2, (June 1, 2011): 145-61 2011.

18 For an alternate translation see Aron Pinker, "Qohelet 4,13-16," in *Scandinavian Journal of the Old Testament* 22.2 (2008):176-194.

19 Rabbinical sources "pairs such as Nimrod and Abraham, Potiphar and Joseph, Saul and David, Pharaoh and Joseph, Nebuchadnezzar and Daniel." See Fox,

sion stands, "it is better to be wise and poor than rich and foolish." Verse 15 introduces another youthful king who leads an even larger number of people. The meaninglessness of the situation is brought about by in the fact that new generations will not appreciate the new, youthful king. Fox affirms, "Though wisdom can bring a poor man to power, he too is quickly succeeded and forgotten. This is senseless."[20]

Ecclesiastes, 30. Ogden asserts that "to deny the possibility of historical allusion in Qoheleth on *a priori* grounds is unacceptable exegetical method." See Graham S. Ogden, "The Historical Allusion in Qoheleth 4:13-16?" in VT 30.3 (1980): 309-315. For the ambiguity of some pronominal suffixes see, Buhlmann, "Thinking in Greek and Speaking in Hebrew (Qoheleth 3:18; 4:13-16; 5:8), in *JSOT* 90 (2000):101-108.

20 Fox, *Ecclesiastes*, 31.

Ecclesiastes 5

5:1-7
Do not bring the sacrifice of fools

5:8-9
Do not be amazed at injustice

5:10-20
Do not love money

5:1-7 Do not bring the sacrifice of fools

5:1-5 Guard your steps when you go to the house of God. To draw near to listen is better than to offer the sacrifice of fools, for they do not know that they are doing evil. Be not rash with your mouth, nor let your heart be hasty to utter a word before God, for God is in heaven and you are on earth. Therefore let your words be few. For a dream comes with much business, and a fool's voice with many words. When you vow a vow to God, do not delay paying it, for he has no pleasure in fools. Pay what you vow. It is better that you should not vow than that you should vow and not pay. Let not your mouth lead you into sin, and do not say before the messenger that it was a mistake. Why should God be angry at your voice and destroy the work of your hands? For when dreams increase and words grow many, there is vanity; but God is the one you must fear.

God takes worship seriously, and so should we. "Guard your steps when you go to the house of God" points to the fact that a measure of care is needed as one approaches God in worship.[1] This care can be seen when one approaches to listen. Not to listen to God's Word as people gather to worship was tantamount to "offer[ing] the sacrifice of fools." Even though done in ignorance, it was considered an evil thing. Verse 2 elaborates on the foolishness of making rash, hasty utterances before God rather than listening.[2] "For God is in heaven and you are on earth," is the reason. Therefore, when the worshiper speaks first and does not listen, he or she takes the place of God in heaven. Trading places with God is not acceptable, thus our words must be few, and our hearts and ears must be wide open to listen to what God has to say. It is implied that the wise listens but the fool talks a lot. "Only a fool prays a lot," concludes Longman.[3] If the worshiper does make a vow in the presence of the LORD, he/she must fulfill that vow. The command to fulfill one's vow is a not a new concept. In the Law, Moses writes,

> If you make a vow to the LORD your God, you shall not delay fulfilling it, for the LORD your God will surely require it of you, and you will be guilty of sin. But if you refrain from vowing, you will not be guilty of sin. You shall be careful to do what has passed your lips, for you have voluntarily vowed to the LORD your God what you have promised with your mouth.[4]

If one does not fulfill one's vow, he or she is rendered a fool. The worshiper must count the cost before making the promise through a vow. Such impertinence draws the anger of God, and He is ready

---

1 Fidler proposes that Qoheleth makes use of the Bethel tradition (Gen 28-35) which becomes "a natural substructure" in the book. See Ruth Fidler, "Qoheleth in "the House of God": Text and Intertext in Qoh 4:17-5:6 (Eng. 5:1-7)" in *Hebrew Studies* 47 (2006), 7-21.

2 The fact that Elohim is used as the name for God "can be understood as Qoheleth's attempt to speak to the universal human condition." See Douglas K. Fletcher, "Ecclesiastes 5:1-7," *Interpretation* 55.3 (2001), 296-298.

3 Longman, *Ecclesiastes*, 152-153.

4 Deuteronomy 23:21-23

to destroy the work of one's hand. While the relationship between increasing dreams and many words is not clear, the main teaching is clear: fear God! The concept of the fear of the LORD does not originate with Solomon, but it is a rather ancient concept that originates in the Mosaic Law. In this case, a man who does not fear God does not watch what he says. Wisdom Literature indeed associates hasty words with foolishness. "Do you see a man who is hasty in his words? There is more hope for a fool than for him" (Prov 29:20). Later in Ecclesiastes, Solomon declares that "a fool multiplies words..." (10:14). As Christians we are reminded of James' exhortation: "everyone should be quick to listen, slow to speak and slow to become angry" (James 1:19).

5:8-9 Do not be amazed at injustice

5:8-9 If you see in a province the oppression of the poor and the violation of justice and righteousness, do not be amazed at the matter, for the high official is watched by a higher, and there are yet higher ones over them. But this is gain for a land in every way: a king committed to cultivated fields.

As Solomon examines life under the sun, he notices that the poor are oppressed, and that justice and righteousness are violated. While some might be surprised by such unethical, immoral behavior, Solomon does not invite his audience to cynicism, nor to a utopian revolution, but to realism. His advice is, "Do not be amazed at the matter" (v. 8). Where bureaucracy reigns supreme, nothing should surprise you. Kidner focuses on the "predatory self-absorption," as officials keep "a baleful eye on the next one down the list...small wonder if the citizen at the bottom of such an edifice found justice a luxury he could not afford."[5] And yet, monarchy is better than anarchy, as long as the king makes provision for the land's farming success.[6]

---

5 Derek Kidner, *The Message of Ecclesiastes* (Downers Grove, Il.,: IVP, 1976), 54-55.

6 Pinker posits that "Ecclesiastes 5:7-8 deals with the inherent value of a central

5:10-20 *Do not love money*

5:10-12 He who loves money will not be satisfied with money, nor he who loves wealth with his income; this also is vanity. When goods increase, they increase who eat them, and what advantage has their owner but to see them with his eyes? Sweet is the sleep of a laborer, whether he eats little or much, but the full stomach of the rich will not let him sleep.

The love of money is not presented as immoral, but as vanity, as meaningless. The meaninglessness of the love of money and wealth is proven in that it does not satisfy, it does not fulfill. The book's conclusion that apart from a correct relationship with God everything is meaningless is proven once again. In chapter 2, Solomon was left empty even though he boasted about his many possessions. Loving money and wealth rather than loving God and/or neighbor is the problem. The New Testament teaching takes this a step further when the Apostle Paul affirms that "the love of money is a root of all kinds of evil" (1 Tim 6:10). Kidner offers a great insight when he states that "man, with eternity in his heart, needs better nourishment than this."[7] For Solomon, the vanity of riches can be seen in their supply and demand. The more supply, the more demand. "When goods increase, they increase who eat them" (v. 11). Thus, he concludes that the owner's only advantage is visual but, while seeing may be believing, it is not fulfilling. Continuing with the wealth motif, Solomon found that sleeping on an empty stomach is better than staying awake because of a full stomach. In contrast with the sweet sleep of the laborer is the implied bitter taste of insomnia. This insomnia is not caused just by food as we can see that the laborer's sleep is sweet, whether his stomach is empty or full. Fox is probably correct when he asserts

---

government headed by a king. While aware of such a system's shortcomings, he emphasizes that the advantage of having a king can be seen in everything." See Aron Pinker, "The Advantage of a Country in Ecclesiastes 5:8," in *Jewish Bible Quarterly* 37.4 (2009), 211-222.

7 Ibid., 56.

that "the insomnia of the rich is induced by worry about losing wealth to others who are trying to consume it."[8]

> *5:13-17 There is a grievous evil that I have seen under the sun: riches were kept by their owner to his hurt, and those riches were lost in a bad venture. And he is father of a son, but he has nothing in his hand. As he came from his mother's womb he shall go again, naked as he came, and shall take nothing for his toil that he may carry away in his hand. This also is a grievous evil: just as he came, so shall he go, and what gain is there to him who toils for the wind? Moreover, all his days he eats in darkness[9] in much vexation and sickness and anger.*

In these verses Solomon identifies two things that are evil: lost wealth (vv. 13-15) and leaving the world with nothing (vv. 16-17). Riches can be detrimental to the one who hoards them, or riches can be lost through a bad venture. Either way, this is seen as a grievous evil.[10] Just as evil is this man's inability to pass on his wealth to his descendants. It is easy to accept the fact that one comes naked into the world, but the idea that one does not get to take to the afterlife what was earned on earth is not only unfulfilling, but it seems unfair. More than that, it seems to be a grievous evil especially since the wealth one accumulates is done "in much vexation and sickness and anger" (v. 17).

> *5:18-20 Behold, what I have seen to be good and fitting is to eat and drink and find enjoyment in all the toil with which one toils under the sun the few days of his life that God has given him, for this is his lot. also to whom God has given wealth and possessions and power to enjoy them, and to accept his lot and rejoice in his toil—this is the gift of God. For he will not much remember the days of his life because God keeps him occupied with joy in his heart.[11]*

---

8 Fox, *Ecclesiastes*, 36.

9 The LXX translates the first part of the verse as, "all his days are in mourning and darkness."

10 Rashbam thinks that the hurt mentioned here refers to the fact that the man is killed or kidnapped for his wealth. See Fox, *Ecclesiastes*, 36.

11 Lofink proposes that God reveals Himself by the joy of the heart. See Norbert Lofink, "Qoheleth 5:17-19—Revelation by Joy," in *Catholic Biblical Quarterly*

After some fairly pessimistic conclusions, Solomon turns to things that are good and beautiful. He praises a life lived in moderation, where eating, drinking, and work are in balance. But we can enjoy these things only because God gives us the life to enjoy them. God is not just the life-Giver but He is the gift-Giver, who graciously gives humanity not just wealth, but the power to enjoy such wealth. The verb translated "occupied" can be translated "answered."[12] If this is the case, then God fills one's heart with joy even though the days of one's life are few.

Reflections from a psychological perspective

As Solomon examines those who are foolish, he seems to be asserting that the fear of God is essential. But how does the fear of God produce wisdom? Conversely, why does a lack of fear produce the foolishness noted in chapter five? Why would God use fear as a method of motivating human beings? Consider that God may have hardwired a fear system into us for the distinct purposes of both survival and learning. There are multiple theories regarding human emotion, and nearly all of them describe fear as one of the most important emotions for motivating people into action.

One such theory is known as the Differential Emotions Theory (Izard, 1991, 1992 and 1993). This theory explains that we have six basic emotions: interest, joy/happiness, anger, sadness, disgust, and fear, which all serve unique motivational purposes. The negative emotion of fear is thought to originate in a brain structure known as the amygdale, which serves the role of aversively motivating the individual to withdraw from whatever environmental stimuli are producing fear (Izard, 2007). Izard argues that fear, along with other basic emotions, blends with the developing human mind to cultivate a complex emotional schema for looking at the world. Thus, the

---

52.4 (1990), 625-635.

12 For a discussion on the two options see George A. Barton, "The Text and Interpretation of Ecclesiastes 5:19," in *JBL* 27.1 (1908): 65-66.

emotion of fear allows us to more effectively learn from our problems. One such example: "So, on the one hand, the desire for sex can recruit an emotion such as interest-excitement and greatly increase sexual motivation, while on the other hand, the presence of fear can inhibit the drive for sex completely."[13] When applied spiritually, fearing the Lord our God permeates our thinking and may make us more effective learners from our environment. Although one may not subscribe to the notion that emotions play such a central role in human development, there is no doubt that the emotion of fear can serve as a powerful teacher and motivator for human behavior.

There appears to be a reoccurring theme in the book of Ecclesiastes whereby Solomon demonstrates how foolishness forms in the hearts of men (5:1-7). He shows how the core beliefs we hold influence our thoughts and the actions that will subsequently follow. In psychology, Beck (1960) led in the development of what is known as Cognitive-Behavioral Treatment (CBT). CBT takes the position that core beliefs influence our current thinking and thus will influence our emotions, physiology, and behavior (see Figure 5.1). Therefore, the goal of CBT is to alter the well-learned patterns of thinking or behavior that are behind people's problems and, by doing so, change the way they feel. CBT is the most widely used form of therapy because it is useful in treating a variety of problems.

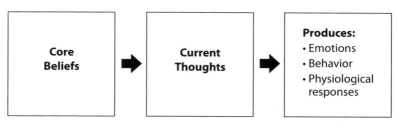

Figure 5:1

---

13 Herbert L. Petri and John M. Govern, Motivation: *Theory, Research and Application,* 6th edition, (Belmont, CA: Wadsworth, Cengage Learning, 2013), 379.

Solomon exhorts us to discipline our minds before God. He also warns us in the Wisdom Literature that we must first fear God (Proverbs 2:5). We are then responsible to be careful and attentive to listen with a heart centered on honoring God through our obedience (Ecc 5:2). In essence, if the heart of the believer is driven by core beliefs that are centered on trusting God, accepting forgiveness of sins, and holding steadfast to the Word of God, then we will take delight in obeying God (Ecc 12:13) and will thus provide hope for the future.

Solomon then proceeds to warn us of the pattern that the foolish will follow. He identifies the core beliefs of the fools who do not humble themselves before God when they approach the house of God (5:1) and do not accept their lowly position before the God of the universe. The fool does not have a healthy fear of the Lord, which in turn leads him or her to impulsive thoughts and actions (5:2-7). The foolish fail to see that because their core beliefs are faulty, they are heading toward impulsive thoughts, feelings, and actions that will have dire consequences (5:1b). The figure below demonstrates the sequence a fool follows and the consequences of his or her behavior (Figure 5.2).

As Solomon states in 5:1-5, when one does not fear God, he or she is hasty to speak and act. Fools will ultimately demonstrate hastiness in their speech, which will produce vows and promises before God and lead them to sin because they will be unable to fulfill what they promise. It is in this hastiness that man has many dreams and plans that do not come to fruition or that fail to satisfy his soul.

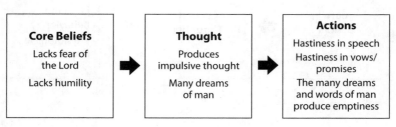

Figure 5:2

Interestingly, Solomon seems to continue this theme of demonstrating a logical sequence of how core beliefs, thoughts, actions, and consequences interact (Figure 5.3). He illustrates the trap of money when one has a false belief that money will satisfy. This false, ungodly belief leads to errors in thinking and then to foolish actions. By tracing behavior backwards, one inevitably will find a false belief that is contrary to fearing God. The classic movie trilogy, *Godfather,* provides a fitting example. The life of the lead character, Michael Corleone, presents a clear depiction of the pursuit of wealth, excess, and strife. Michael Corleone is able to amass large amounts of wealth through many illegal practices as well as through the legalization of gambling in Nevada. He spends most of his life trying to protect the family fortune while seeking to secure a financial future for his empire. His monetary pursuits, his association with organized crime, and his absence from his family cost him two marriages, countless damaged relationships, and the death of two siblings and one child, and his own exile to a Sicilian villa. In the final scene of the Godfather trilogy, Michael Corleone is sitting by himself in a chair in front of his Sicilian villa where he dies alone and essentially forgotten.

Belief: That money will provide satisfaction for the soul			
It will not satisfy the strivings of man's heart	**Thoughts: Love of money and fear of losing it**		
Ecc 2:22-23	Ecc 5:10-11: The constant rumination on money and abundance does not bring the satisfaction that was hoped for but the fool still holds on to the belief that money and abundance will ease the strivings of the heart.	**Actions: Hoarding, worry, and pain**	
Ecc 7:29 "Behold, I have found only this, that God has made men upright, but they have sought out many devices."		The constant rumination seen in Ecc 5:10-11 produces a more desperate pursuit of money. The inability of abundance to satisfy causes the fool to be willing even to take increasing risk (Ecc: 5:14- bad investment) in the hope that increased wealth will eventually satisfy the soul.	**Consequences/Rewards**
			Your own hurt (vexation, sickness, anger, and worry over losing the money/abundance that you seek) Being alone because you are seeking wealth and thus eat in darkness and if you lose the money no one will be there to take care for you. Finally the ultimate reality that even if you keep money, you can't take it with you.

Figure 5:3

Conclusion 5:18-20

In his conclusion to this chapter, Solomon offers a fresh perspective on how to view money and abundance (Figure 5.4). The Preacher teaches that we must believe that we have to first enjoy what God has given and not hold on to the false hope that money and abundance will satisfy our souls. He further asserts that as one fears and obeys God, each individual can take enjoyment in drinking, eating, and having intimate relationships. Solomon concludes that we are then free to experience life with gladness in our hearts as a reward.

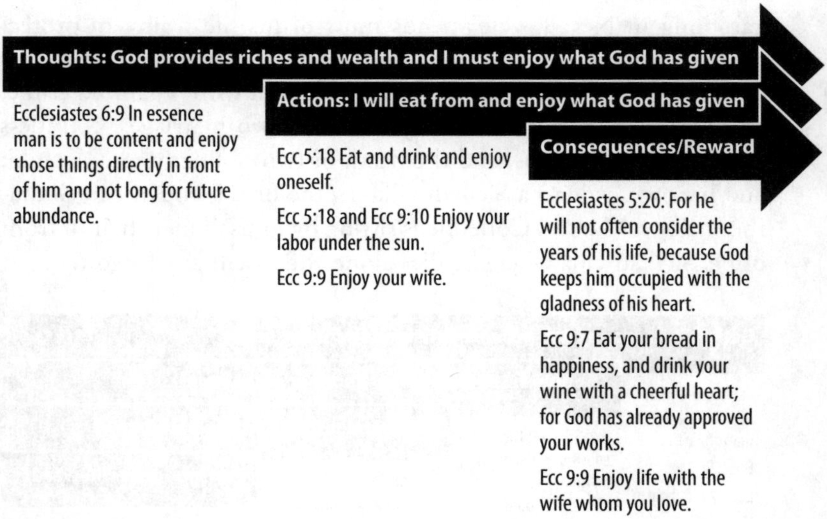

Thoughts: God provides riches and wealth and I must enjoy what God has given

Ecclesiastes 6:9 In essence man is to be content and enjoy those things directly in front of him and not long for future abundance.

Actions: I will eat from and enjoy what God has given

Ecc 5:18 Eat and drink and enjoy oneself.

Ecc 5:18 and Ecc 9:10 Enjoy your labor under the sun.

Ecc 9:9 Enjoy your wife.

Consequences/Reward

Ecclesiastes 5:20: For he will not often consider the years of his life, because God keeps him occupied with the gladness of his heart.

Ecc 9:7 Eat your bread in happiness, and drink your wine with a cheerful heart; for God has already approved your works.

Ecc 9:9 Enjoy life with the wife whom you love.

Figure 5:4

Ecclesiastes 6

6:1-6
*Apart from a correct relationship with God,
riches will not fulfill one.*

6:7-9
*Apart from a correct relationship with God,
labor will not satisfy.*

6:10-12
*Apart from a correct relationship with God,
simple questions will have no answers.*

6:1-6 Apart from a correct relationship with God, riches will not fulfill one.

> *6:1-2 There is an evil that I have seen under the sun, and it lies heavy on mankind: a man to whom God gives wealth, possessions, and honor, so that he lacks nothing of all that he desires, yet God does not give him power to enjoy them, but a stranger enjoys them. This is vanity; it is a grievous evil.*

Three times in Ecclesiastes Solomon affirms that "there is an evil" which he sees "under the sun."[1] The scenario that is labeled "evil" here in 6:1 has to do with a man that has been given wealth, possessions, and honor by God. What is evil is the fact that this person, for whatever unspecified reasons, is not given the power to enjoy these very sought-after things. Even worse, a stranger enjoys them. Is

---

1 The expression appears four times in Ecclesiastes (5:13, 16; 6:1; 10:5), but only three of these appear in conjunction with "under the sun" (5:13; 6:1; 10:5).

Solomon speaking of himself or someone else? The text does not say, so to speculate would be improper. And yet, Solomon affirms God's sovereignty. It is God who gives wealth, possessions, and honor, and it is God who gives or withholds the power of one to enjoy them. Can a Christ-follower consider it evil when someone else has these blessings? A godly person would not mind if someone else is blessed with wealth, possessions, and honor. Thus, a godly person would consider this as meaningful, not meaningless. A godly person would rejoice with those who rejoice, and would not see someone's prosperity as a grievous evil.[2]

> *6:3-6 If a man fathers a hundred children and lives many years, so that the days of his years are many, but his soul is not satisfied with life's good things, and he also has no burial, I say that a stillborn child is better off than he. For it comes in vanity and goes in darkness, and in darkness its name is covered. Moreover, it has not seen the sun or known anything, yet it finds rest rather than he. Even though he should live a thousand years twice over, yet enjoy no good-- do not all go to the one place?*

If anyone could have 100 children it would be the man with 700 wives and 300 concubines, but here, Solomon is probably thinking hypothetically.[3] He is thinking about both life and death. Lack of satisfaction in life and a lack of burial in death would lead one to conclude that everything is meaningless. But Qoheleth goes a step further to suggest that "a stillborn child is better off" than a graveless corpse. Covering one's name in darkness "is idiomatic for non-existence or death; the name is the person."[4] While pro-abor-

---

2 Maussion sees "glory" and "allow" as two key words. "Consequently, one is able to find some explanations using the opposition between luxurious pleasure and honest joy." See Marie Maussion, "Qohélet 6:1-2: 'Dieu Ne Permet Pas...'" in VT 55.4 (2005): 501-510.

3 Pinker suggests the following reading, "If a man begets a hundred, and lives many years, and of much power would be the days of his years, but his gullet is not sated of the good, and also a burial he did not have, I say: the stillborn is better off than he." See Aron Pinker, "The Ligature שׁ =אֹ in Qoheleth 6:3," *Bible Translator* 62.3 (2011): 151-164

4 Murphy, *Ecclesiastes*, 54.

tion advocates would want to use this verse to bolster their culture of death, that is not what the verse says. Verse 5 clarifies that "rest" is the standard. Barrick writes, "miscarriage 'knows' nothing of the frustrations, disappointments, and enigmas of the life under the sun. 'It is better than he' should be translated more literally, 'more rest has this one than that one.'"[5] Even though the Torah states that a long life is a blessing from God as a result of honoring one's parents (Exod 20:12), Solomon implies, via a rhetorical question, that a long life without enjoyment is meaningless. This is a drastic change from the view of a long life that is viewed as a reward for the wise, as related in the book of Proverbs.[6] Apart from a correct relationship with God, one can only conclude that death renders everything meaningless. For the follower of Christ, however, death is described as "sleep,"[7] and to be absent from the body is to be present with the Lord.[8] And there is nothing meaningless about that.

6:7-9 *Apart from a correct relationship with God, labor will not satisfy.*

6:7-9 All the toil of man is for his mouth, yet his appetite is not satisfied. For what advantage has the wise man over the fool? And what does the poor man have who knows how to conduct himself before the living? Better is the sight of the eyes than the wandering of the appetite: this also is vanity and a striving after wind.

In chapter 2 Solomon affirmed that he did not find satisfaction in laughter, women, wine, wealth, or building projects. He now generalizes the idea that work won't satisfy because it's aimed at short-term fulfillment. It only goes as far as one's mouth.[9] The rhetorical ques-

---

5 Barrick, *Ecclesiastes*, 106.

6 Proverbs 3:16, 18; 4:10; 28:16.

7 "Behold! I tell you a mystery. We shall not all sleep, but we shall all be changed…" (1 Cor 15:51).

8 "Yes, we are of good courage, and we would rather be away from the body and at home with the Lord" (2 Cor 5:8).

9 Pinker recommends the following rendition, "Better the sight of the eyes, then

tion "what advantage has the wise man over the fool?" points to the fact that one's craving is not satisfied whether one is wise or a fool. While the wise seems to have no advantage over the fool in this case, the second part of verse 8 seems to suggest the same for the poor who knows how to conduct himself. Solomon seems to get on the instant gratification wagon, affirming that "better is the sight of the eyes than the wandering of the appetite." Consequently, he reverts back to his pessimistic refrain, "This is also vanity/meaningless and a striving after wind." Indeed, apart from a correct relationship with God, work will not satisfy.

6:10-12 *Apart from a correct relationship with God, simple questions will have no answers.*

6:10-12 Whatever has come to be has already been named, and it is known what man is, and that he is not able to dispute with one stronger than he. The more words, the more vanity, and what is the advantage to man? For who knows what is good for man while he lives the few days of his vain life, which he passes like a shadow? For who can tell man what will be after him under the sun?

Is the naming of things referring to Adam's naming the living creatures back at the beginning of creation?[10] Possibly.[11] But the second part of verse 10 seems to contrast the limitation of humanity with the omnipotence of God. The One who is stronger is God, and Solomon accepts this truism. Fox compares and contrasts Job and Qoheleth:

---

what goes in the throat. That too, vapour, and chasing of wind." See Aron Pinker, "Qohelet 6:9 – It Looks Better than it Tastes," in *Journal of Jewish Studies* 60.2 (2009):214-225.

10 "Now out of the ground the Lord God had formed every beast of the field and every bird of the heavens and brought them to the man to see what he would call them. And whatever the man called every living creature, that was its name" (Gen 2:19). Some scholars erroneously correlate this verse with the beginning of the Enuma Elish. See Barton, *Ecclesiastes*, 136 and Gordis, *Koheleth*, 262-263.

11 Garrett sees a literary allusion to Genesis 2:19. See Garrett, *Proverbs, Ecclesiastes and Song of Songs*, 317.

Koheleth's outlook contrasts with that of Job, who believes that if he could confront God, there might be a change—and if not a change, at least an explanation; Koheleth expects neither. Silence in the fear of God (6:10b–11; 5:5; 3:14b) is the only prudent behavior in a world in which humans can do little (6:10a; 3:14–15) and understand less (6:12; 3:11).[12]

If one does speak, more words won't produce more answers, but rather more vanity, more meaninglessness. And if humanity cannot take pride in its feebleness, it cannot boast in its transience either. Not only is the length of one's life "like a shadow,"[13] from a qualitative perspective, for Solomon, one's life is vain, meaningless. The rhetorical questions, "Who knows?" and "Who can tell?" demand the answers, "Nobody knows," and "Nobody can tell," but that is only true for the one who knows that God exists, yet consistently and systematically disobeys God.[14] For the godly, Bible-believing follower of Christ, the answers to these questions are "God knows," and "God can tell." After all, the Bible presents God as all-knowing; there is nothing hidden from Him. At the end of the book, Solomon will see the proverbial light and will rightly conclude that what humanity should do is "Fear God and keep His commandments."[15]

Reflections from a psychological perspective

The field of positive psychology, despite its more humanistic roots, has begun to shed interesting scientific light on the pursuit of happiness, and in part, the role of wealth in society. As a body of literature, several trends in the research are worthy of discussion. One notable

---

12 Michael V. Fox, *Ecclesiastes*, 42.

13 Ecclesiastes 8:13 once again confirms that the days of one's life are "like a shadow."

14 Wise suggests that Qoheleth seems "to quote a popular proverb and then comment on it." See Michael O. Wise, "A Calque from Aramaic in Qoheleth 6:12, 7:12, 8:13)," *Journal of Biblical Literature* 109.2 (1990): 249-257.

15 "The end of the matter; all has been heard. Fear God and keep his commandments, for this is the whole duty of man" (Ecc 12:13).

trend globally is that among the wealthiest nations there is no increase in life satisfaction, despite an ever increasing buying power.[16] Research supports the idea that money and possessions do not increase life satisfaction. Solomon apparently learned similar lessons through numerous building projects and unmatched accumulation of wealth in the history of Israel. To further illustrate this point, a study of the Forbes Top 100 wealthiest people showed that they failed to experience any more happiness than the average American.[17]

---

16 Martin E. P. Seligman, *Authentic Happiness,* 50-55."source":"Open World-Cat","event-place":"New York","abstract":"Publisher description: Positive Psychology focuses on strengths rather than weaknesses, asserting that happiness is not the result of good genes or luck. Seligman teaches readers that happiness can be cultivated by identifying and using many of the strengths and traits that they already possess -- including kindness, originality, humor, optimism, and generosity. By frequently calling upon their \"signature strengths\" in all the crucial realms of life, readers will not only develop natural buffers against misfortune and the experience of negative emotion, they will move their lives up to a new, more positive plane. Drawing on groundbreaking psychological research, Seligman shows how Positive Psychology is shifting the profession's paradigm away from its narrow-minded focus on pathology, victimology, and mental illness to positive emotion, virtue and strength, and positive institutions. Seligman provides the Signature Strengths Survey along with a variety of brief tests that can be used to measure how much positive emotion readers experience, in order to help determine what their highest strengths are.","ISBN":"0743222989 9780743222983","shortTitle":"Authentic happiness","language":"English","author":[{"family":"Seligman","given":"Martin E. P"}],"issued":{"date-parts":[[["2004"]]}}}],"schema":"https://github.com/citation-style-language/schema/raw/master/csl-citation.json"}

17 Ibid."source":"Open WorldCat","event-place":"New York","abstract":"Publisher description: Positive Psychology focuses on strengths rather than weaknesses, asserting that happiness is not the result of good genes or luck. Seligman teaches readers that happiness can be cultivated by identifying and using many of the strengths and traits that they already possess -- including kindness, originality, humor, optimism, and generosity. By frequently calling upon their \"signature strengths\" in all the crucial realms of life, readers will not only develop natural buffers against misfortune and the experience of negative emotion, they will move their lives up to a new, more positive plane. Drawing on groundbreaking psychological research, Seligman shows how Positive Psychology is shifting the profession's paradigm away from its narrow-minded focus on pathology, victimology, and mental illness to positive emotion, virtue and strength, and positive institutions. Seligman provides the Signature Strengths Survey along with a variety of brief tests that can be used to measure how much positive emotion readers experience, in order to help determine what their highest strengths are.","ISBN":"0743222989 9780743222983","shortTitle":"Authentic happiness","language":"English","author":[{"family":"Seligman","given":"Martin E. P"}],"issued":{"-

So, does money have any correlation to happiness? As it pertains to happiness, evidence appears to support the idea that wealth increases happiness only if the person is experiencing significant poverty. Therefore, we can determine that wealth is illusive at best and does not increase our happiness; wealth increases happiness only in so far as the person's basic needs are met.

Solomon illustrates in Ecc 6:2 that despite man's receiving all that he desires in the form of wealth, possessions, and honor, he will not be able to enjoy them. Is this Solomon circling around (Ecc ch. 2) to the disappointing realization that neither possessions, wealth, nor honor will bring lasting satisfaction? Had he set his mind on obtaining these items and found that after considerable effort to obtain them that there would be no rich enjoyment in these things late in his life? Solomon states that God does not give man the power to enjoy riches. But is this his frustration that all these were never designed by God to produce happiness? Perhaps Benjamin Franklin stated it best when he said, "Money has never made man happy, nor will it; there is nothing in its nature to produce happiness. The more of it one has the more one wants."[18] Even though wealth will not increase our happiness, is Solomon compelling us to find enjoyment in our work under the sun?

God's design for work was established from the beginning of mankind (Genesis 2:15; 1:26-31). Even after sin entered the world (Gen 3:17-19), our work was for both our enjoyment and satisfaction (Ecc 5:18-19). However, our labor was never intended to be the central focus or to replace where our real meaning and purpose come from (Ecc 12:13-14; Col 3:17 and 1 Corinthians 10:31). Psychological research regarding work has found some revealing insights. The term "calling" is often used in the literature to describe the intrinsic value of work and is correlated strongly with the concept of a sense of fulfillment for both oneself and the larger world. Wrzesniewski found that these calling orientations are strong predictors of whether someone wanted to spend more time at work and also correlate

date-parts":[["2004"]]}}}],"schema":"https://github.com/citation-style-language/schema/raw/master/csl-citation.json"}

18 Benjamin Franklin at BrainyQuote, brainyquote.com

with satisfaction and enjoyment.[19] Earlier in both Ecclesiastes 3:12-13 and 5:18-19 Solomon states that work can be enjoyed when we first grasp that work is God's gift to us. Furthermore, the Scriptures identify that all work must be done with His glory in mind. (Ecc 12:13-14, Colossians 3:17). A definite consistency is apparent regarding biblical concepts and psychological literature. It also appears that those with a calling in a career or with a purpose to their career are more likely to work harder even to the point of doing it for less pay.[20] Research supports that a calling may have a wider impact than previously noted as researchers have found that career purpose can even promote optimism.[21]

Solomon utilizes the rhetorical question (6:12) to bring us back to the realization that we do not have the answers in this life. He further asserts that it is a grievous mistake to think otherwise. As most clinical psychologists, pastors, and social workers will tell you, they have seen countless individuals who have placed their careers over more meaningful activities such as a relationship with God and family. Wong and Fry found that life satisfaction and happiness are actually tied to a strong sense of meaning while a lack of meaning is in turn predictive of disengagement and depression.[22] This disappointing realization comes crashing in only when they lose their jobs, wives, and families. Sadly it's only then that many realize that money, possessions, and honor were truly chasing after the wind. First Timothy 6: 9-10 states, "But those who desire to be rich fall into temptation, into a snare, into many senseless and harmful de-

---

19 A. Wresniewski, C. R. McCauley, P. Rozin, and B. Schwartz, "Jobs, Careers and Callings: People's Relations to Their Work," *Journal of Research in Personality* 31, no. 1 (1997): 21-33

20 Ibid.

21 Jane E. Gillham, Andrew J. Shatté, Karen J Reivich, and E.P., "Optimism, Pessimism, and Explanatory Style." In *Optimism & Pessimism: Implications for Theory, Research, and Practice,* 53-75. referenced in Corey L. M. Keyes and Jonathan Haidt, eds, *Flourishing: Positive Psychology and the Life Well-Lived,* 1st edition, (Washington, DC: American Psychological Association, 2003), 190.

22 Wong and Fry, *The Human Quest for Meaning: Theories, Research, and Application,* referenced in Corey L. M. Keyes and Jonathan Haidt, eds. *Flourishing: Positive Psychology and the Life Well-Lived,* 107–108.

sires that plunge people into ruin and destruction. For the love of money is a root of all kinds of evils. It is through this craving that some have wandered away from the faith and pierced themselves with many pangs."

Ecclesiastes 7

7:1-14
Wisdom is better than folly.

7:15-29
Miscellaneous reflections on righteousness, justice, and evil

7:1-14 Wisdom is better than folly.

The beginning of chapter seven resembles the book of Proverbs. The "better than" sayings are a key feature in wisdom literature. The similarities between this chapter and the book of Proverbs could be strong evidence of Solomonic authorship for both Proverbs and Ecclesiastes.

> *7:1-4 A good name is better than precious ointment, and the day of death than the day of birth. It is better to go to the house of mourning than to go to the house of feasting, for this is the end of all mankind, and the living will lay it to heart. Sorrow is better than laughter, for by sadness of face the heart is made glad. The heart of the wise is in the house of mourning, but the heart of fools is in the house of mirth.*

"A good name is better than precious ointment" is similar to Proverbs 22:1, "A good name is to be chosen rather than great riches."

Someone's name points to his/her reputation. Just like an ointment's fragrance is spread around, so one's reputation can be a blessing to those around him.[1] Ben Sira's insight is great, "Take care of your name, for it will remain for you longer than a thousand stores of gold. The goodness of life lasts only for a few days, but the goodness of a name lasts forever."[2] While the first "better/than" saying can be easily understood, the second is more difficult. Why would someone's death day be better than his/her birthday? After all, we celebrate one's birthday, but mourn one's death day. It could be that Solomon praises the death day for the one who found no meaning or satisfaction in a God-fearing, meaningful life.

Verses 2-4 continue the idea of the end of verse 1 for "there is much to be gained by sober reflection on death."[3] While verse 1 does not tell why a good name is better than precious ointment, or why the death day is better than the birthday, verse 2 gives us the reason that mourning is better than laughter and feasting: because "the living will lay it to heart." While food at a feast goes through the stomach, sober reflection goes through the heart. Indeed, death reminds us both that we are finite, and thus our earthly pilgrimage comes to an end (v. 2). If one's death day is better than one's birthday, Solomon concludes that "sorrow is better than laughter, for by sadness of face the heart is made glad." The Hebrew text sets the contrast between good and bad/evil: "For in badness/evil of face the heart is made good." Subsequently, the wise will seek to be at a funeral rather than a banquet hall. The wise and the fool are compared and contrasted. Both have a heart, but one seeks a place where the heart will contemplate while the other seeks a place where the heart seeks enjoyment. Fox remarks, "the wise, knowing life's futility, are melancholy (1:18), while fools have a good time."[4]

---

1 "Banqueters in the ancient world were often treated by a generous host to fine oils that would be used to anoint their foreheads. This provided not only a glistening sheen to their countenance but also would have added a fragrance to their persons and the room." See Walton, Matthews, and Chavalas, *The IVP Bible Background Commentary* (Downers Grove, IL: IVP, 1997), 573.

2 Sir 41:12-13 as quoted in Seow, *Ecclesiastes*, AYB, 235

3 Garrett, Proverbs, Ecclesiastes, *Song of Songs,* 318.

4 Fox, *Ecclesiastes*, JPS, 45. Longman suggests that the fool lives without the end in

*7:5-6 It is better for a man to hear the rebuke of the wise
than to hear the song of fools. For as the crackling of thorns
under a pot, so is the laughter of the fools; this also is vanity.*

In the book of Psalms, God is the one who rebukes (Ps 9:5, 119:21).
Here, the wise serve as God's agents to rebuke the ones who need it.
This rebuke is better than the song of fools. It could be that this song
is a song of praise, but it is contrasted with a wise rebuke. Thus, this
song of fools is "meaningless and grating."[5] The saying in verse 6 is
"onomatopoeic…the word sirim ("thorns") puns on sir ("kettle")."[6]
The laughter of fools is as irritating as the crackling of thorns on fire.
The laughter of fools provides no instruction or edification, just like
thorns on fire produce no heat. They are both useless.

*7:7-9 Surely oppression drives the wise into madness, and a bribe
corrupts the heart. Better is the end of a thing than its beginning, and
the patient in spirit is better than the proud in spirit. Be not quick in
your spirit to become angry, for anger lodges in the heart of fools.*

The word translated "oppression" can also be translated "cheating,"
or "dishonest."[7] Neither cheating nor receiving bribes should be part
of the wise lifestyle. If cheating creeps into one's life, the wise one becomes a fool. The teaching against taking bribes is not original with
Solomon. In the Torah, Moses wrote, "You shall not pervert justice.
You shall not show partiality, and you shall not accept a bribe, for a
bribe blinds the eyes of the wise and subverts the cause of the righteous."[8] Longman concludes that "one of the effects of the verse is to
show that even wisdom is not foolproof."[9]

Verse 8 seems to be out of context, but it could correlate with
the overall theme of death. The idea that the end is better than the

---

sight. See Longman, *Ecclesiastes*, 184.

5 Fox, *Ecclesiastes*, JPS, 45.

6 Ibid. Bullinger identifies the figure of speech as paronomasia. Bullinger, *Figures
of Speech Used in the Bible*, 545.

7 Lev 6:4, Psalm 62:10.

8 Deut 16:19.

9 Longman, *Ecclesiastes*, 185.

beginning could be a repetition of the second part of verse 1 which asserted that one's death day is better than one's birthday. Krüger argues that this verse stands in contrast with verses 1-6 and it "encourages confidence that the outcome of a matter will be better than its beginning."[10] The last part of verse 8 contrasts the patient and the proud. While the opposite of pride is humility, that humility can be demonstrated through patience. Indeed, wisdom literature always associates the fool with anger and lack of patience, while the wise is patient.[11] Subsequently, Solomon shifts to a direct, immediate command, "Do not be quick in your spirit to become angry."[12] The danger of anger is that it is not transient, but it "lodges in the heart of fools." In contrast with the fool, the wise one is "neither naïve nor cynical and embittered."[13]

> *7:10-14 Say not, "Why were the former days better than these?" For it is not from wisdom that you ask this. Wisdom is good with an inheritance, an advantage to those who see the sun. For the protection of wisdom is like the protection of money, and the advantage of knowledge is that wisdom preserves the life of him who has it. Consider the work of God: who can make straight what he has made crooked? In the day of prosperity be joyful, and in the day of adversity consider: God has made the one as well as the other, so that man may not find out anything that will be after him.*

The myth of the "good ol' days" is not a 21st century invention. Solomon's contemporaries were just as tempted as we are to think that living in the past was better, that grass was greener in a previous decade, that sin didn't do as much damage as today. It is foolish to deny the reality of the present and to be naïve about history.[14] It seems that for Solomon, there was such a thing as a foolish question.

---

10 Krüger, *Qoheleth*, 137.

11 Bullinger describes the relationship between "spirit" and "anger" as a metonymy of the cause.

12 See Allen P. Ross, *Introducing Biblical Hebrew* (Grand Rapids: Baker, 2001), 152 for the negation of the jussive as immediate, negative command.

13 Garrett, *Proverbs, Ecclesiastes, Song of Songs,* 320.

14 Longman, *Ecclesiastes,* 189.

That question was, "Why was yesterday better than today?" Even if the past was better than the present, it is not wise to ask the question. Rather, verse 14 gives the answer: if the days are good, rejoice; if the days are days of adversity, mediate, think, and consider that all days are a gift from God.

Verses 11 and 12 affirm the value and advantage of wisdom. "Wisdom is good with an inheritance" seems to be an obvious statement.[15] Garrett observes, "Even the wise prefer prosperity to poverty. Those who possess both money and wisdom are under the protection of both."[16] Verse 12 advances the idea that wisdom combined with wealth provides protection for the wise. However, it is only wisdom that is still present in one's daily adversity and preserves the wise one's life. Wisdom then, is the currency of endless worth.

Since life includes both days of prosperity and days of adversity, one needs to approach life joyfully when thing go well, and introspectively when days are hard. The word translated "consider" appears in verses 13 and 14. Humanity is encouraged to consider what God has done. While verse 13 emphasizes that we cannot undo what God has done, verse 14 affirms God's sovereignty even if our days are full of adversity. It would be foolish for us to challenge the Sovereign God who has created all things and who sustains all things. It would be wiser if we would just submit to His authority rather than challenge His ways.[17]

7:15-29 Miscellaneous reflections on righteousness, justice, and evil

7:15-18 In my vain life I have seen everything. There is a righteous man who perishes in his righteousness, and there is a wicked man who

---

15 Some suggest that a better translation is "wisdom is as good as an inheritance." See Longman, *Ecclesiastes*, 189-190.

16 Garrett, *Proverbs, Ecclesiastes, Song of Songs*, 321.

17 Pinker suggests that 7:13 needs "to be understood in a general sense, as an expression of a fundamental law of nature, irreversibility. Irreversibility has practical and moral implications. It is thus a natural component of Kohelet's worldview." See Aron Pinker, "The Principle of Irreversibility in Kohelet 1,15 and 7,13," *ZAW* 120 (2008): 387-403.

prolongs his life in his evildoing. Be not overly righteous, and do not make yourself too wise. Why should you destroy yourself? Be not overly wicked, neither be a fool. Why should you die before your time? It is good that you should take hold of this, and from that withhold not your hand, for the one who fears God shall come out from both of them.

Life lived away from God is classified as vain and meaningless.[18] In his disappointment, Solomon exaggerates and affirms that he has seen everything. He sees what his father saw, too, namely that sometimes the wicked outlive the righteous. His disappointment clouds his judgment. Thus, he wrongly implies that one can be too righteous or too wise. Not only that, but living too righteously or too wisely might bring about one's untimely death. This concept does not fit with the Wisdom Literature's teaching that righteousness and wisdom prolong one's life.[19] Some suggest that Solomon is warning against being a fanatic,[20] or that "this is not an exhortation to do a little sinning,"[21] but rather that he is dealing with one's "philosophy of life that seeks the benefits of long life, prosperity, and personal happiness through the strict observing of religious and wisdom principles."[22] On the other hand, one can be overly wicked and a fool. Later New Testament revelation concurs that one's sinful lifestyle can hasten one's death day.[23] Solomon correctly concludes that the fear of the Lord is what one needs in order to live a balanced life.[24]

---

18 The word translated "vain" here is the same word that is translated "meaningless" in other parts of Ecclesiastes.

19 Proverbs 3:16 "Long life is in [wisdom's] right hand; in her left hand are riches and honor."

20 Garrett, *Proverbs, Ecclesiastes, Song of Songs,* 323.

21 J. A. Loader, *Polar Structures in the Book of Qohelet* (Berlin: Walter de Gruyter, 1970), 48.

22 Garrett, *Proverbs, Ecclesiastes, Song of Songs,* 323. See also, Wayne A. Brindle, "Righteousness and Wickedness in Ecclesiastes 7:15-18," in Andrews University Seminary Studies, 23.3 (1985): 243-257.

23 1 John 5:16

24 Murphy argues that "Qoheleth's view is that neither virtue nor folly achieves certain results in life, and one does well to attend to the failure of zealots in both areas." See Roland E. Murphy, "On Translating Ecclesiastes," CBQ 53 (1991): 571-579. Shnider and Zaleman argue that for Qohelet wisdom and righteousness "don't necessarily mix very well; but, if you keep a grip on the fundamental

> *7:19-22 Wisdom gives strength to the wise man more than ten rulers who are in a city. Surely there is not a righteous man on earth who does good and never sins. Do not take to heart all the things that people say, lest you hear your servant cursing you. Your heart knows that many times you yourself have cursed others.*

The superiority of wisdom is a key theme in Wisdom Literature, but this is the first place where wisdom is said to add to the physical strength of a man.[25] Longman sees wisdom here as being portrayed as the most important of human quality or ability.[26] The total power of ten rulers in one place would amount to an insurmountable level, but this would pale in the face of the strength of God-given wisdom. Verse 20 is a theologically rich verse that points to the limitations of one's abilities. Sin gets in the way. The Reformers would later call this concept "original sin," and/or "total depravity." Indeed, the only man who was fully righteous and never sinned was Jesus the Messiah.[27] But this is not just a New Testament teaching. Proverbs 8:12-14 affirms that wise, godly living stands in stark contrast with foolish, wicked living. The wise one fears the Lord and consequently he/she has both strength and insight. In contrast with the wise, the fool is proud, arrogant, and his foolishness can be detected even in his speech. Curses[28] are part of the speech of the wicked, but the wise must not take these words to heart. One's heart is the internal witness that reminds everyone that no one is innocent of this sin of the heart and tongue.

---

principles of basic morality and common sense and don't overdo things, you can hold on to both." See Steve Shnider and Lawrence Zalcman, "The Righteous Sage: Pleonasm or Oxymoron? (Kohelet 7,16-18)," *ZAW* 115 (2003): 435-439.

25 In Psalm 89:17 the word translated "strength" refers to physical strength.

26 Longman, *Ecclesiastes*, 198.

27 Hebrews 4:15. The Old Testament classifies Noah as "righteous" (Gen 6:9), and the presence of righteous people is affirmed throughout the Old Testament (Job 17:9; Ps 5:12, 11:3, 34:17; Prov 2:20, 3:33, 10:6; Isa 26:7: Jer 20:12, Ezek 3:20, 18:5; Amos 2:6; Hab 1:4, 2:4). Yes, these righteous people were not sinless.

28 The word translated "cursing" comes from the Hebrew llq and can be translated "to slander, to belittle."

> *7:23-28 All this I have tested by wisdom. I said, "I will be wise,"*
> *but it was far from me. That which has been is far off, and deep,*
> *very deep; who can find it out? I turned my heart to know and to*
> *search out and to seek wisdom and the scheme of things, and to*
> *know the wickedness of folly and the foolishness that is madness.*
> *And I find something more bitter than death: the woman whose*
> *heart is snares and nets, and whose hands are fetters. He who*
> *pleases God escapes her, but the sinner is taken by her. Behold,*
> *this is what I found, says the Preacher, while adding one thing to*
> *another to find the scheme of things—which my soul has sought*
> *repeatedly, but I have not found. One man among a thousand I*
> *found, but a woman among all these I have not found.*

The compound "all this" could refer to the section preceding or following this introductory phrase, or it could refer to both. Krüger affirms that wisdom is both the "instrument" and "object" of the text.[29] Solomon laments that wisdom was far from him, and that the place of wisdom is in a very deep, deep place. But that was not always the case. 1 Kings 4:29 affirms that "God gave Solomon wisdom and understanding beyond measure." What brought Solomon to the place of lament was his consistent and systematic disobedience to the God who appeared to him twice (1 Kgs 3:5; 9:2). The main theological point of the book is reiterated: Apart from a correct relationship with God everything is meaningless, and one will be left empty and unfulfilled despite his/her prestige, power, and possessions. Surprisingly, even though he had 1,000 women, he found that more bitter than death is "the woman whose heart is snares and nets, and whose hands are fetters." Is Solomon talking about the same woman who Moses declared was created in the image of God?[30] Is he talking about women in general or does he have a certain woman in mind?[31] Gordis harshly asserts that Koheleth expresses his distrust of women. "Their physical charms (her hands, v. 26) and their emotional appeal

---

29 Krüger, *Qoheleth*, 144.

30 Genesis 1:26 -27.

31 Some scholars suggest that the adjective "bitter" refers to the experience not a woman. See R.B.Y. Scott. *Proverbs. Ecclesiastes.* AB (Garden City, NY: Doubleday, 1965), 239.

(her heart, v. 26) are alike dangerous to man, because honor, rare among men, is non-existent among women."[32] Zimmermann, on the other hand, suggests that the verse describes Qoheleth's relationship with his wife. "He has criminal thoughts and death wishes toward her; the words 'death' and 'wife' are collocated together. She is full of traps (deception) and she is choking him."[33] Kaiser proposes that the woman is the "strange woman" found in Proverbs 1-9.[34] If so, it makes sense that the one who pleases God is delivered, but the sinner falls into her trap.

In his search Solomon does find something that would label him a misogynist. "One man among a thousand I found, but a woman among all these I have not found" (7:28). Barton tries to bury him by stating that "he is more than reflecting the Oriental view that women are more prone to sin than men…Qohelet is saying that perfect men are rare, perfect women are non-existent."[35] Keddie tries to defend him by stating that the poetic language should not be taken dogmatically. Rather, Qoheleth's "poetic statistics for the relative uprightness of men and women cannot be meant to draw any serious comparison between the two."[36] Is this the worldview of a God-fearing man? Is this the view we must have today? The answer is an emphatic, "No!" Jesus died and rose again to redeem us from the meaninglessness Solomon experienced. Jesus said, "I came that they may have life and have it abundantly" (John 10:10). Women should be viewed as made in the image of God (Gen 1:26-27), and as wives, women are classified as good (Prov 18:22). Our view of humanity needs to be corrected by wearing our Christological spectacles, seeing people from the perspective of Jesus who died and rose again so that we can have forgiveness of sin and eternal life with Him.

---

32 R. Gordis, *Koheleth: The Man and His World* (New York: Schocken, 1968), 282.

33 Frank Zimmermann, *The Inner World of Qohelet* (New York: KTAV, 1973), 152.

34 Kaiser, *Quality Living* (Chicago: Moody, 1979), 110.

35 G.A. Barton, *Ecclesiastes*, ICC (Edinburgh: T & T Clark, 1959), 147.

36 Gordon J. Keddie, *Looking for the Good Life: The Search for Fulfillment in the Light of Ecclesiastes* (Phillipsburgh, NJ: Presbyterian & Reformed Pub Co, 1991), 99.

7:29 See, this alone I found, that God made man upright,
but they have sought out many schemes.

Solomon correctly concludes that even though humans were created upright, they became corrupt. Longman sees this verse as "an obvious reflection on the first few chapters of Genesis where God pronounces the results to be very good."[37] Gordis suggests that the last verse of chapter 7 should be taken as a reference to human perversity as a whole, pointing out that evil is not God's will, but man's doing.[38] Eaton concurs, "The blame for the rarity of wisdom is attributed to no one but mankind himself. He was created neither sinful, nor neutral, but upright, a word used of the state of the heart which is disposed to faithfulness or obedience."[39]

Reflections from a psychological perspective

"God whispers to us in our pleasures, speaks in our
conscience, but shouts in our pains: it is His megaphone to
rouse a deaf world." C. S. Lewis[40]

Solomon in the following chapter further pushes us to wrestle with concepts such as death, reputation, balanced living, the pursuit of wisdom, and reverent humility. As Solomon opens this chapter, we see the value of reputation and its importance as one considers death. In the house of mourning we learn to value this life and gain a perspective that our time on earth is short lived. The realization of our own death calls our current decisions into question. We must also acknowledge that we will be held accountable for our actions (Ecc 12:14). Furthermore, we must also acknowledge that the pursuit of wisdom is far better than the lifestyle of a fool.

---

37 Longman, *Ecclesiastes*, 207.

38 Gordis, *Koheleth*, 285.

39 M.A. Eaton, *Ecclesiastes* (Leicester: IVP, 1983), 116. See also, Michael V. Fox and Bezalel Porten, "Unsought Discoveries: Qohelet 7:23-8:1a," in *Hebrew Studies* 19 (1978): 26-38.

40 C. S. Lewis, *The Problem of Pain* (New York: Simon & Schuster, 1996), 83

Although one cannot rely on psychological literature to determine what is considered wise in the world's eyes, there are still some fascinating correlations. Staudinger et al. found that wisdom was most frequently correlated with social intelligence, psychological maturity, fewer mental health problems, sociability, open-mindedness, and even-temperedness.[41] In another longitudinal study, researchers found that wisdom predicted better transition into menopause for women ten years in advance.[42] Furthermore, the research on wisdom found no correlation between life's problems (dark days) and life satisfaction.[43] Ardelt found that those who experienced troubles actually showed increased wisdom compared with those who did not experience hardships.[44] This would suggest that to the wise person circumstances are opportunities for growth and not necessarily barriers to life.[45] One variable that appears very important in developing wisdom in the psychological literature is ego resilience: how one finds meaning and purpose during stressful times.[46] This sheds very interesting light on verse 14 when Solomon states, "In the day of prosperity be joyful, and in the day of adversity consider: God has made the one as well as the other, so that man may not find out anything that will be after him." Solomon is affirming that we must trust in the sovereignty of God if we want to handle adversity well.

Balanced Living as it pertains to your faith
(Ecclesiastes 7:15-18)

As believers, we know to flee evil. But in verse 16, Solomon advises the reader to not be overly righteous. The question that exists is

---

41 Staudinger, Lopez, and Baltes, "The Psychometric Location of Wisdom-Related Performance: Intelligence, Personality, and More?" referenced in Christopher Peterson and Martin Seligman, *Character Strengths and Virtues* (American Psychological Association / Oxford University Press, 2004), 189.

42 Hartman, "Women Developing Wisdom: Antecedents and Correlates in a Longitudinal Sample," referenced in Peterson and Seligman, *Character Strengths and Virtues*, 185-193.

43 Monika Ardelt, 2001, "Social Crisis and Individual Growth: The Long-Term Effects of the Great Depression," *Journal of Aging Studies* 12, no. 3: 291-314.

44 Ibid.

45 Hartman, 185-193

46 Hartman, 185-193

whether someone can be so theologically driven that he/she could begin to miss the application component of their faith? In Matthew we see the seven woes that are pronounced on the Pharisees and Sadducees (Matt. 23:1-38). There we find that some people hold their faith dogmatically in a way to seek after the approval of others and for their own personal benefit. Religious dogmatism is demonstrated by intolerance, a closed system of thought, perceiving others as a threat, being overly righteous, and having a narrow perspective that is resistant to change.[47] Previous research has found a consistent relationship between dogmatism and neuroticism.[48] It is worth consideration that individuals who hold their faith in dogmatic ways may be less likely to display social interest and more likely to display behaviors or attitudes associated with neuroticism. As other researchers have proposed, the dogmatic or rigid individual may appear close-minded due to anxiousness or defensive structures that ward off personal threat, insecurity, and uncertainty.[49] One could propose that this anxiety or defensive posturing produces a religious individual who is concerned with self-preservation and consequently is less concerned with others.

In contrast to religious dogmatism, social interest involves tolerance and may be best represented by the "one another" statements of Scripture. Adlerian theory considers social interest a core concept in Individual Psychology. Ansbacher and Ansbacher identified social interest as the single most important human quality.[50] Social interest has long been thought of in Adlerian theory as a sign of psycho-

---

47 M. Rokeach, "The Nature and Meaning of Dogmatism," Psychology, 61, (1954), 194-204

48 L. J. Francis, "Dogmatism and Eysenck's Two-Demensional Model of Personality Revisited," *Personality & Individual Differences,* 24, (1998): 571-573.; P. G. Schmitz, "Sociocultural and Personality Differences in the Dimension of the Open and Closed Mind," *High School Journal,* (1985): 348-364.; M. A. Thalbourne, K. A. Dunbar and P. S. Delin, "An Investigation into correlations of belief in the paranormal," *Journal of the American Society for Psychical Research,* 89 (1995): 215-231.

49 L. J. Francis, "Dogmatism and Eysenck's Two-Demensional Model of Personality Revisited," 571-573; P. G. Schmitz, "Sociocultural and Personality Differences in the Dimension of the Open and Closed Mind," 348-364.

50 H. L. Ansbacher and R. R. Ansbacher, eds., 1956, *The Individual Psychology of Alfred Adler,* (New York: Basic Books, 1956), 133-142.

logical maturity and mental health.[51] Dinkmeyer, Dinkmeyer, and Sperry stated, "Adlerians believe that mental health can be measured in terms of one's social interest, the willingness to participate in the give and take of life and to cooperate with others and be concerned about their welfare."[52] Social interest in this way may aid in the development of psychological maturity or wisdom and thus help people strike a balance between a sinful human nature and the human longing to connect with others.

Based on the research of Roberts among dogmatic religious individuals there exists a strong relationship between their level of dogmatism and social interest scores. Dogmatism manifests itself in being less cooperative or having interactions with others marked by less warmth and consequently less social interest.[53] Roberts found that dogmatic religious individuals may display a distrust of others, increased anxiety, and less warmth in interacting with others and less social interest or, better stated, the one another statements of Scripture.[54] Thus a dogmatic individual may experience more difficulty in interpersonal relationships where warmth and trust are considered desirable. In Ecclesiastes, Solomon seems to conclude that we must enjoy our life and be troubled by winning the approval of others by looking more righteous than others, i.e. having the outside of the cup clean (Matthew 23:25-26).

Does a balanced life in faith mean that one avoids the religious dogmatism of the Pharisees and Sadducees? Is following the customs or traditions of one's faith at times just a to-do list to get a desired reward, such as the praise of others? Is the pursuit of one's faith in a rigid manner at times to avoid the unpredictable nature of human relationships? Or is a reverent humility that is based on a healthy fear

51 M. H. Bickhard and B. L. Ford, 1976, "Adler's Concept of Social Interest: A Critical Explication, *"Journal of Individual Psychology"* 32, no. 1: 27-49.

52 D. C. Dinkmeyer, D. C. Dinkmeyer, Jr, and L. Sperry, *Adlerian Counseling and Psychotherapy,* (Columbus: Merrill Publishing Co, 1987).

53 Kevin W. Roberts, "Dogmatism Viewed Multivariately in Predicting the Level of Social Interest among Biblical Studies Students." PsyD diss, Adler School of Professional Psychology, 2003, 62-96.

54 Ibid.

of God necessary for someone to seek after God for the purpose of bringing glory to God and not themselves?

> Then Jesus said to the crowds and to his disciples, "The scribes and the Pharisees sit on Moses' seat, so do and observe whatever they tell you, but not the works they do. For they preach, but do not practice. They tie up heavy burdens, hard to bear, and lay them on people's shoulders, but they themselves are not willing to move them with their finger. They do all their deeds to be seen by others. For they make their phylacteries broad and their fringes long, and they love the place of honor at feasts and the best seats in the synagogues and greetings in the marketplaces and being called rabbi by others. But you are not to be called rabbi, for you have one teacher, and you are all brothers. And call no man your father on earth, for you have one Father, who is in heaven. Neither be called instructors, for you have one instructor, the Christ. The greatest among you shall be your servant. Whoever exalts himself will be humbled, and whoever humbles himself will be exalted (Matthew 23:1-12).

So what does it mean to be humble? Tangey did a comprehensive review of literature on humility and has revealed a composite definition including: the ability to acknowledge one's mistakes, limitations, and imperfections, an improved awareness of personal abilities, and an increased ability to "forget the self" as well as the contributions of others to the world.[55] They also demonstrate an openness to new ideas and the ability to effectively manage complex information which initially seems contradictory and is accompanied by more frequent references for the need of a Higher Power.[56]

A humble person will demonstrate an increased ability to look at one's mistakes and thus is more likely to offer and seek forgiveness from others.[57] For the mark of fools is that they cannot receive the

---

55 J. P. Tangney, "Humility," in *Handbook of Positive Psychology,* edited by C. R. Snyder and S. J. Lopez, (New York: Oxford University Press, 2002), 483-90.
56 Ibid.
57 Michael E. McCullough, Everett L. Worthington Jr., and Kenneth C. Rachal,

correction necessary because they lack the humility to hear the truth about themselves (Ecc 7:5). Exline, Baumeister, Faber, and Holland found that people who saw themselves as morally similar rather than superior over others were far more likely to forgive others.[58] Does humility then keep us in touch with our own depravity?

A humble view of self that lacks disparaging comments is also related to improved self-regulation efforts and often leads to a more stable view of oneself because he or she is not consumed with maintaining a public image to others.[59] This openness to personal image may aid the humble person in being able to critically self-evaluate and thus be more likely to set self-improvement goals.[60] Does this relate to his point in Ecclesiastes 7:8, "Better is the end of a thing than its beginning, and the patient in spirit is better than the proud

---

"Interpersonal Forgiving in Close Relationships" *Journal of Personality and Social Psychology* 73, no. 2 (1997): 321-36

58 Exline et al., "Can Admitting Weakness Be a Strength? Seeing One's Capability for a Similar Misdeed Predicts Forgiveness." References in Peterson and Seligman, *Character Strengths and Virtues,* 468.

59 Weiss and Knight, "The Utility of Humility: Self-Esteem, Information Search, and Problem-Solving Efficiency," referenced in Peterson and Seligman, *Character Strengths and Virtues,* 470.

60 Heine et al., "Divergent Consequences of Success and Failure in Japan and North America."North Americans who failed on a task persisted less on a follow-up task than those who succeeded. In contrast, Japanese who failed persisted more than those who succeeded. The Japanese pattern is evidence for a self-improving orientation: Failures highlight where corrective efforts are needed. Japanese who failed also enhanced the importance and the diagnosticity of the task compared with those who succeeded, whereas North Americans did the opposite. Study 2 revealed that self-improving motivations are specific to the tasks on which one receives feedback. Study 3 unpackaged the cultural differences by demonstrating that they are due, at least in part, to divergent lay theories regarding the utility of effort. Study 4 addressed the problem of comparing cultures on subjective Likert scales and replicated the findings with a different measure.","ISSN":"0022-3514","note":"PMID: 11642348","shortTitle":"Divergent consequences of success and failure in japan and north america","journalAbbreviation":"J Pers Soc Psychol","language":"eng","author":[{"family":"Heine","given":"S. J."},{"family":"Lehman","given":"D. R."},{"family":"Ide","given":"E."},{"family":"Leung","given":"C."},{"family":"Kitayama","given":"S."},{"family":"Takata","given":"T."},{"family":"Matsumoto","given":"H."}],"issued":{"date-parts":[["2001",10]]},"PMID":"11642348"}}],"schema":"https://github.com/citation-style-language/schema/raw/master/csl-citation.json"} referenced in Peterson and Seligman, *Character Strengths and Virtues,* 469–470.

in spirit"? "Be not quick in your spirit to become angry, for anger lodges in the heart of fools" (v. 9). Does the person who is "patient in spirit" or humble understand his own depravity and choose to take a realistic and honest view of himself? Does this realistic or honest view that is no longer consumed with maintaining a public image better able to admit what it does not know or understand?

Solomon ends chapter seven by discussing the depth of complexity of life under the sun. Despite the wisdom given to him by God (1 Kings 3:11-14), Solomon repeatedly expresses his uncertainty over "the deep, very deep" things in life. Solomon spent considerable time trying to understand the scheme of things "which my soul has sought repeatedly, but I have not found." Was this a glimpse of the humility that we saw in the promising young ruler's prayer in 1 Kings 3:7-9? If this book was written near the end of his life, is it possible he has finally accepted his limitations of understanding and the wisdom of his choices? Solomon concludes that "God made man upright" but that human desires and schemes show the depth of our sin. As a follower of Christ, we should first understand the depth of our own sin and as a result discover a reverent humility and desperate dependency upon God.

Ecclesiastes 8

8:1-6
The supremacy of the king

8:7-8
The limits of human knowledge

8:9-17
The supremacy of God

8:1-6 The supremacy of the king

> 8:1 Who is like the wise? And who knows the
> interpretation of a thing? A man's wisdom makes his face
> shine, and the hardness of his face is changed.

This transitional verse affirms the benefits of wisdom.[1] While some questions remain unanswered, wisdom still benefits one's demeanor. In Old Testament times, the shining of one's face was associated with divine presence and blessing. Moses' face shone after being in the presence of Yahweh (Exod 34:30). "The LORD make his face to shine upon you," was the priestly blessing associated with the children of Israel (Num 6:25). Ben Sira affirmed that "the sign of a good heart

---

1 Contra Longman suggests that verse 1 is a "sarcastic exclamation of frustration that stands between two larger units," Longman, Ecclesiastes, 208. For an argument of the unified literary composition of 8:1-9 see Scott C. Jones, "Qohelet's Courtly Wisdom: Ecclesiastes 8:1-9," in *CBQ* 68.2 (2006):211-228.

is a shining face."[2] Wisdom, however, does not exempt one from hard times. But the presence of wisdom again proves beneficial as "the hardness of his face is changed" even in the midst of trials and hardships.

> *8:2-6 I say: Keep the king's command, because of God's oath to him. Be not hasty to go from his presence. Do not take your stand in an evil cause,3 for he does whatever he pleases. For the word of the king is supreme, and who may say to him, "What are you doing?" Whoever keeps a command will know no evil thing, and the wise heart will know the proper time and the just way. For there is a time and a way for everything, although man's trouble lies heavy on him.*

Submission to authority is a main theme throughout the Scriptures.[4] The motivation for obeying the king is not because he earned the people's respect, but because of the oath he swore in God's name. The faithful should always be model citizens, no matter who the king is since God is the Sovereign one, overseeing all matters under the sun. Once in the presence of the king, do not desire to leave quickly.[5] When you do take a stance, make sure you are on the side of good and of the king. The motivation is not because it is the right thing to do, but because the king "does whatever he pleases."[6] It is implied that the king is just and will act on the side of good and not evil. More than that, the king's word is "supreme," and nobody can question him. This was not the time of separation of powers and multiple branches of government. Checks and balances were not yet created. This was the time of the monarchy, and the king's actions seemed to have gone uncontested. Verse 5 summarizes the idea that

---

2 Fox, *Ecclesiastes*, 54.

3 Waldman argues that in light of Akkadian material, this verse "has the contextual background of plotting against the king and rebelling against him." See Nahum M. Waldman, "The *dābār ra'* of Ecc 8:3," in *JBL* 98.3 (1979):407-408.

4 The Apostle Paul expands on this topic in Romans 13.

5 Another variant reads, "Do not be stupefied at his presence." See Seow, *Ecclesiastes*, 280.

6 The question "What are you doing?" is used also in Job 9:12 and Isaiah 45:9 but there the Sovereign One is God.

the wise person has a "wise heart," and subsequently he/she discerns the "proper time" and "just" way of doing things. "There is a time and a way for everything" seems to be another way of saying "For everything there is a season, and a time for every matter under heaven" (Ecc 3:1). The word "everything" includes "man's trouble." Even though one may live wisely in relationship to God, the king, and others, one is not exempt from trouble. Even so, obedience leads to a richer and fuller life.[7]

8:7-8 The limits of human knowledge

8:7-8 For he does not know what is to be, for who can tell him how it will be? No man has power to retain the spirit, or power over the day of death. There is no discharge from war, nor will wickedness deliver those who are given to it.

No matter how wise or knowledgeable one is, only God knows the future. Verse 7 can be the "Amen" of verse 6, but one thing is for sure, namely, human knowledge is limited only to the past and present. Since God is not limited by time and space, he knows the past, present, and future. Human knowledge is limited, and Solomon laments the fact that no human has control over one's life or his lifespan. Solomon employs the language of war to emphasize that this is a war one cannot avoid, and this is one war one cannot win. Is he being fatalistic? I think not. I think he is just being realistic. God is the sovereign Creator and Sustainer of all; He is the limitless One.

8:9-17 The supremacy of God

8:9-13 All this I observed while applying my heart to all that is done under the sun, when man had power over man to his hurt. Then I saw the wicked buried. They used to go in and out of the holy place and were praised in the city where they had done

---

7 Fox, *Ecclesiastes*, 55. For the difficult language of verse 10 see Chaim W. Reines, "Koheleth 8:10," in *Journal of Jewish Studies* 5:3 (1954): 86-87.

> *such things. This also is meaningless. Because the sentence against
> an evil deed is not executed speedily, the heart of the children of
> man is fully set to do evil. Though a sinner does evil a hundred
> times and prolongs his life, yet I know that it will be well with
> those who fear God, because they fear before him. But it will not
> be well with the wicked, neither will he prolong his days like a
> shadow, because he does not fear before God.*

Verse 9 seems to be a link between the section that ended with verse
8 and the one that starts in verse 10. Like his father David, Solomon saw the vanity and futility of the wicked having a fancy burial.
Although though they flaunted their wickedness even in the "holy
place," they were praised both in life and death. Solomon repeats
his refrain, "This is also meaningless!" The Law of Moses promised
blessings to the righteous and curses to the wicked.[8] But in Solomon's
observation, the scales of justice were not working properly. The one
who was supposed to be rebuked for his/her wicked deeds was praised
instead. In Solomon's estimation, this is futile and meaningless.

Verse 11 explains why there is such a vast amount of evil present.
"Because the sentence against an evil deed is not executed speedily"
is the reason given for one's heart to be "fully set to do evil." If the
judicial system is slow or broken, those who break the law go from
bad to worse.[9] Is there then any advantage to being righteous? In the
end, Solomon asserts that for "those who fear God" things "will be
well." Kidner suggests that "this could mean that whereas the godly
man has hope beyond the grave, the ungodly has none: however long
postponed, death will be the end for him."[10] Furthermore, the life of
the wicked is "like a shadow," all show but no substance. Kidner's
insight can serve as a good summary of this section, "Wickedness
digs its own grave, and righteousness, so to speak, its own garden."[11]

---

8 Deuteronomy 28. See also Aron Pinker, "The Doings of the Wicked in Qohelet,"
in *Journal of Hebrew Scriptures* 8 (2008): 1-22, J. J. Serrano, "I Saw the Wicked
Buried (Ecclesiastes 8:10)," in CBQ 16.2 (1954):168-170, and Kay Weißflog,
"Worum geht es in Kohelet 8,10," *Biblische Notizen* 131 (2006):39-45.

9 Those who deny Solomonic authorship of Ecclesiastes ask, "If Solomon was
king, why didn't he do something about this slow and/or broken system?"

10 Kidner, *The Message of Ecclesiastes*, 77.

11 Kidner, 78. Sneed argues that 8:12b-13 represents the "author's own sentiment

*8:14-17 There is a vanity that takes place on earth, that there
are righteous people to whom it happens according to the deeds
of the wicked, and there are wicked people to whom it happens
according to the deeds of the righteous. I said that this also is
vanity. And I commend joy, for man has nothing better under
the sun but to eat and drink and be joyful, for this will go with
him in his toil through the days of his life that God has given
him under the sun. When I applied my heart to know wisdom,
and to see the business that is done on earth, how neither day
nor night do one's eyes see sleep, then I saw all the work of God,
that man cannot find out the work that is done under the sun.
However much man may toil in seeking, he will not find it out.
Even though a wise man claims to know, he cannot find it out.*

Verse 14 begins and ends with the word translated "vanity," "meaningless," "futile." If we use the blessings/curses language of the Torah,
it does not make sense for the righteous to get the curses meant for
the wicked, and for the wicked to benefit from the blessings promised to the righteous. And yet, as Solomon observes how things take
place "on earth," this is exactly the case. And yet, he does not digress
into fatalism; rather, he chooses to see the brighter side of life. "Joy"
can be experienced in the middle of the mundane eating and drinking of everyday life.[12] This is the third time he appeals to the Carpe
Diem dictum.[13]

Solomon's search was thorough but tiresome. Sleepless nights
did not give way to clear answers. One thing did come into sharper
focus, however: God is the Sovereign Creator. Even though humanity is on a search to fully understand what God is doing, "man cannot
find out the work that is done under the sun." If Solomon is speaking
about himself, then he "is declaring his own inability to understand
absurdities such as the injustices described in 8:10–14. The failure of
wisdom to penetrate the world's paradoxes is just another of life's in-

---

and signifies that he does not absolutely reject the deed/consequence connection."
See Mark Sneed, "A Note on Qoh 8:12b-13," in *Biblica* 84 (2003):412-416.

12 See Graham S. Ogden, "Qoheleth's Use of the 'Nothing is Better' – Form," in
JBL 98.3 (1979):339-350.

13 The other two Carpe Diems are in 2:24-26 and 5:18-20.

equities."[14] So Shakespeare's Hamlet was wrong in thinking that life is a tale told by an idiot, but "what if it is told to an idiot?"[15] There are limits to human knowledge and wisdom. Did God put on these limits at creation? Or, are these limitations the natural results of the fall? We cannot know. It is best to surrender to the God who does know all. Kinder challenges us that "as time-dwellers we see God's work in tantalizing flashes, the very fact that we can ask about the whole design and long to see it, is evidence that we are not entirely prisoners of our world. In more promising words, it is evidence of not only how but for Whom we have been made."[16]

Reflections from a psychological perspective

There are many events in this life that are difficult to understand, including when bad things happen to good people and when good things happen to those who do evil (Ecc 8:14). For many of us, the unpredictability or lack of control of these events often produces fear and anxiety. Fear is used in Scripture in different forms including respect and awe. The fear of the LORD is the beginning of all knowledge (Proverbs 1:7, 29; Ecc 12:13). However, anxiety tends to be focused on personal desires for control and is often projected into the future (8:6, 16-17). As seen in those verses, anxiety can cause sleepless nights. Whereas fear may motivate us to action, we know that anxiety produces both heaviness of heart and that it will ultimately provide no relief to any situation (Prov 12:25; Job 6:2-3). In fact, Proverbs 24:19-20 and Psalm 37:1-9 tell us that anxiety is linked to envy, jealousy, and even manipulation.

Solomon lays out a basic human problem of accepting what we can and cannot control as we toil under the sun. The unpredictability of events is not only difficult to understand but is often beyond our control. Solomon illustrates this in v. 8, "No man has power to retain the spirit, or power over the day of death. There is no discharge from

---

14 Fox, *Ecclesiastes*, 61.

15 Kidner, 79.

16 Ibid.

war, nor will wickedness deliver those who are given to it." In essence, Solomon may be indicating that we are helpless to predict nature, our lives, or our dealing with others including our superiors. But this is a difficult concept for many of us to accept. Instead, when dealing with others, we prefer to practice something called external control psychology. William Glasser first introduced the idea that people use external control psychology to get the people in their lives to do things they don't want to do.[17] In an effort to control our environment, Glasser believes that we practice this basic psychology: "Punish the people who are doing wrong, so they will do what we say is right; then reward them, so they keep doing what we want them to do."[18]

If human beings do not accept their own limitations and humbly trust in the sovereignty of God (Ecc 12:13), they are left with very few options. Some individuals will exhibit their anxiety by attempting to plan out all possible scenarios in their lives as a way to soothe the fear they experience. Others will try to control those closest to them as a way of protecting themselves or others from harm. We may also experience a desire to control others as a personal attempt to relieve our anxiety. This line of thinking is practiced every day as a pervasive pattern of resolving situations that seem beyond our control. Is this what Solomon is referring to when he references the "schemes" of man (Ecc 7:29)? Solomon addresses this issue of control and the fact that justice is not always delivered to those who do evil (Ecc 8:11). He instructs us that even though we cannot understand or control our environment, that is not to be our focus (8:12). Instead he counsels that if we fear God and obey His commands, wisdom will be given to us.

In the field of secular psychology there are many different theories of the causes of anxiety. Some of them include genetic, social, and environmental factors that contribute to its manifestation. However, Manaster and Corsini (1982) provide a summary of the work of Alfred Adler who used the following diagram to illustrate the cause of anxiety.[19]

---

17 Glasser, *Choice Theory.*
18 Ibid, 5.
19 Manaster and Corsini, *Individual Psychology*), 109.

If What is = What should be…Contentment
If What is > What should be…..Satisfaction
If What is < What should be….Anxiety

In this model, if a person sees a discrepancy between how they are and how they should be, then anxiety is the by-product. For example, if a student sees himself as lacking the adequate intelligence to be in college and he is given a large and difficult assignment, then anxiety is the result of this felt discrepancy.

This chapter of Ecclesiastes, offers a different solution for dealing with one's seemingly uncontrollable and sometimes unjust environment than experiencing anxiety. Solomon seems to support the notion that we must first accept the reality of our own finite human wisdom and understanding. In Ecclesiastes 3:11 and 8:17 we are instructed that we cannot understand God's plan from the beginning all the way to the end. Although many of us intellectually understand that God has the power of life and death, we often have difficulty accepting and embracing this truth. Instead of accepting model A (see below) those who fear God and obey his commands can rest in the sovereignty of God in response to their fear (Psalm 34:4, Psalm 56:3-4, Psalm 139:23-25). Instead of allowing anxiety to weigh heavily upon us, we find that His consolation can bring great relief and joy to our souls (Psalm 94:18-19, 2 Corinthians 7:5-7). As seen in the New Testament (2 Corinthians 6:10), joy is a much richer form of happiness, despite unknown circumstances. The Scriptures promise us that deep joy can be found in following God's commands because these paths are the ones God has set for us (Ecc 8:15). As a result we are now instead free to experience the joy and peace promised in Scriptures despite our disappointments with our current reality (Ecc 8:1 & 8:15).

A. If What is < What should be….Anxiety = attempts to control our environment.

B. If What is < What should be = choosing to trust/fear God and rest in the sovereignty of God (Isaiah 26:3-4, Psalm 139:16)

Ecclesiastes 9

9:1-10
Lessons of life and death

9:11-12
Lessons from irony

9:13-18
Lessons from history

9:1-10 Lessons of life and death

9:1 But all this I laid to heart, examining it all, how the righteous and the wise and their deeds are in the hand of God. Whether it is love or hate, man does not know; both are before him.

Solomon emphasizes again the powerful doctrines of God's sovereignty and omniscience. The love/hate dichotomy in the Old Testament can be about acceptance/rejection and not just emotions. Whichever Solomon has in mind we cannot know, but that is not relevant. What matters is that God knows when we love or hate.[1] That is not to say that He approves of hating other people. In light of New Testament revelation, the faithful are called to love our enemies and pray for those who persecute us.[2]

---

1 "There is a time to love and a time to hate" (Ecc 3:8), but this is not an imperative. Rather, as he explored things under the sun, he saw that people both love and hate others. He is not making moral pronouncements suggesting that people should hate other people.

2 Matthew 5:44.

9:2-3 It is the same for all, since the same event happens to the righteous and the wicked, to the good and the evil, to the clean and the unclean, to him who sacrifices and him who does not sacrifice. As the good one is, so is the sinner, and he who swears is as he who shuns an oath. This is an evil in all that is done under the sun, that the same event happens to all. Also, the hearts of the children of man are full of evil, and madness is in their hearts while they live, and after that they go to the dead.

The universal nature and knowledge of death is not a new insight. But Solomon laments the fact that both the righteous and the wicked die. The righteous are classified as good partly because they bring sacrifices and make vows. It is assumed here that they live in obedience to the sacrificial system as outlined in the Law of Moses. The wicked do not bring sacrifices and they are classified as "sinners" who "shun an oath." They are not interested in what the Law of God says, or to live according to His will as revealed in the Law. Even so, death is referred to as "the same event" that "happens to all." Solomon concludes that this is not only not good, but that this is, in fact, the absence of good; it is "evil." How does this fit with his view of God's sovereignty? It seems that it doesn't. But he is not afraid to ask the tough questions and even to allow the life/death question to remain in an unresolved tension.

9:4-6 But he who is joined with all the living has hope, for a living dog is better than a dead lion. For the living know that they will die, but the dead know nothing, and they have no more reward, for the memory of them is forgotten. Their love and their hate and their envy have already perished, and forever they have no more share in all that is done under the sun.

Even though life and death are realities for both the wicked and the righteous, there is a clear advantage to those who are in the land of the living. The living have hope[3]! Life is worth living because of hope! The text does not specify anything about this hope, but Kaiser suggests that the living have "the hope of preparation for meet-

---

3 The word can also be translated "hope," "trust," or "confidence."

ing God," "the hope of living significantly," and the "hope of doing something to the glory of God."[4] The advantage of the living is also seen in the expectation of a reward. Those who die bury with them love, hate, and envy, and they join in the underworld as they leave the land of those living "under the sun."

> *9:7-10 Go, eat your bread with joy, and drink your wine with a merry heart, for God has already approved what you do. Let your garments be always white. Let not oil be lacking on your head. Enjoy life with the wife whom you love,5 all the days of your vain life that he has given you under the sun, because that is your portion in life and in your toil at which you toil under the sun. Whatever your hand finds to do, do it with your might, for there is no work or thought or knowledge or wisdom in Sheol, to which you are going.*

So what is one to do "under the sun?" "Eat, drink," and be "merry!" But these every day, mundane activities are to be done differently from the way the one with no hope does them. Eating should be accompanied by joy.[6] Drinking should be accompanied by a merry heart. Joy and merriness do not originate with food or drink, but rather with the understanding that God has already approved what you do. Calvin Miller speaks about the Pharisees during the time of Jesus and their lack of joy. "The Pharisees were especially stern with their religion. Their laughter was so infrequent that if you saw a Pharisee doubled over in laughter, you marked the day and hour. The Pharisees served a stern God. This God from time to time shouted down over the balustrades of heaven, 'Are you having a good time?' If ever a Pharisee felt inclined to answer, 'Yes, God, we are!' then their God would shout back, 'Well, stop it! Are you religious leaders or not?' "[7]

---

4 Kaiser, *Ecclesiastes*, 97.

5 See Johan Yeong Sik Pahk, "A Syntactical and Contextual Consideration of '*sh* in Qoh. XI 9," *VT* 51.3 (2001): 370-380.

6 Pinker suggests that 9:3b-7 is a polemic against necromancy (the practice of communicating with the dead). See Aron Pinker, "Qohelet 9:3b-7: A Polemic against Necromancy," *Journal of Jewish Studies* 63.2 (2012): 218-237.

7 Calvin Miller, *Until He Comes* (Nashville: Broadman and Holman, 1998), 48.

Enjoyment of life in ancient Israel could have included wearing white clothes[8] and anointing oneself with oils. White could symbolize "purity, festivity, or elevated social status,"[9] while anointing oneself with oils goes back to ancient Egypt.[10] Fox attests that some Rabbis "taught that the clean clothes and oil represent good deeds and Torah, whereby we keep ourselves morally ready for God's 'banquet' on the day of our death."[11]

9:11-12 *Lessons from irony*

> *9:11-12 Again I saw that under the sun the race is not to the swift, nor the battle to the strong, nor bread to the wise, nor riches to the intelligent, nor favor to those with knowledge, but time and chance happen to them all. For man does not know his time. Like fish that are taken in an evil net, and like birds that are caught in a snare, so the children of man are snared at an evil time, when it suddenly falls upon them.*

Solomon is talking about life in ironic terms. He observed that sometimes races are not won by the swiftest, the war is not won by the strongest, food is not earned by the wisest, riches do not end up in the house of the intelligent, favor is not earned by those with knowledge. Rather, all of them are bound by time and chance. "Merit is not always rewarded, and the world can be unfair. Wisdom, skill, and hard work can promote but not guarantee success,"[12] concludes Garrett. The irony of ironies is that "man does not know his time." Death comes indeed

---

8 Boyle suggests that "for Qoheleth the real problem is the divine silence and the inscrutability of the divine design." See Brian Boyle, "'Let Your Garments Always Be White' (Ecc 9:8): Time, Fate, Chance and Provident Design According to Qoheleth," *Austrailia Biblical Review* 55 (2007): 29-40.

9 Longman, *Ecclesiastes*, 230.

10 The ancient Egyptians practiced anointing for cosmetic purposes. See "Anoint, Anointed," in the *Baker Encyclopedia of the Bible,* edited by Walter A. Elwell and Barry J. Beitzel (Grand Rapids: Baker, 1988), 116.

11 Fox, *Ecclesiastes*, 63. See also Jean-Jacques Lavoie, "Bonheur et Finitude Humaine: Étude de Qo 9, 7-10," Science et Espirit 45 (1993): 313-324.

12 Garrett, *Proverbs, Ecclesiastes, Song of Songs,* 332.

like a thief in the night, unexpectedly. Fox suggests that "Koheleth turns from ordinary mishaps to the great misfortune, death, which falls upon people suddenly, like a net."[13] Indeed, the wisdom of humanity is to realize that we are indeed only one heartbeat away from eternity.[14]

9:13-18 Lessons from history

> *9:13-18 I have also seen this example of wisdom under the sun, and it seemed great to me. There was a little city with few men in it, and a great king came against it and besieged it, building great siegeworks against it. But there was found in it a poor, wise man, and he by his wisdom delivered the city. Yet no one remembered that poor man. But I say that wisdom is better than might, though the poor man's wisdom is despised and his words are not heard. The words of the wise heard in quiet are better than the shouting of a ruler among fools. Wisdom is better than weapons of war, but one sinner destroys much good.*

Solomon's history lesson points again to the superiority of wisdom. A poor, wise man is of more value than an (unwise) great king. We are not told the methods used by the poor, wise man to deliver the city, Solomon concludes that "wisdom is better than might" even if this wisdom is not valued or appreciated. Just because his words are not popular doesn't mean they are not wise. Furthermore, "the words of the wise heard in quiet are better than the shouting of a ruler among fools." Indeed, shouting is not a sign of power, rather, it is a sign of weakness. Quiet, wise words are more powerful and thus more useful then shouting foolish ones. The employment of wisdom in war is better military strategy than the use of weapons. Unfortunately, "the brilliant plans of a leader, faithfully followed by many, have been brought to nothing by the stupid incompetence of one man."[15]

---

13 Fox, *Ecclesiastes*, 65.

14 Lavoie suggests that for Qoheleth, justice is a utopian reality with God being the one controlling one's fate. See Jean-Jacques Lavoie, "Temps et Finitude Humaine: Étude de Qohélet IX 11-12," *VT* 46.4 (1996): 439-447.

15 Barton, *Ecclesiastes*, 165-166. Joshua 7:1-26 is an excellent example of how the sin of Achan brought the defeat of the entire Israelite army.

Reflections from a psychological perspective

The Sovereignty of God and the Depravity of Man

There appears to be a pattern in Solomon's writing that follows a logical progression. First and foremost, Solomon stresses the sovereignty of God and that mankind cannot figure out God's ways (Ecc 3:14-15 and 9:1). He further teaches that man is both depraved and fragile in this life and destined for death. As difficult as this is to hear, we must all accept the inevitable reality that we will die. Solomon cleverly addresses the issue that each of us is destined to meet the same fate (Ecc 9:2-3). However, we tend to focus on the future at hand and not on the ominous reality of what is to come. Can we even be certain about our future tomorrow? And the rhetorical answer is of course not, for neither you nor I can add a single day to our lives. So what point is Solomon driving home?

Some may view this as a pessimistic outlook. Among psychological theories this would most likely line up the closest with the existential theories. However, Solomon moves beyond the existential counseling theories by instructing us to recognize our own frailty and to continually keep our minds focused on God. He goes even further to say that we are to "enjoy life" or "see life" in light of gifts that God has given to us. The existentialist counseling theories hold that people are left to make meaning out of their own world.[16] Solomon's perspective moves far beyond the existentialist viewpoint regarding our inevitable death, and encourages us to live a life of meaning and purpose, enjoying God's rich blessing.

Does embracing death provide us with the freedom necessary to live a life with more joy? Solomon identifies six areas of enjoyment, namely, food, drink, marriage, comfort, clothing, and work (Ecc 9:7-9). Abraham Maslow was a psychologist and philosopher in the late 1950s who developed a theory to explain human motivation and striving. Interestingly, Solomon's six areas correspond with

---

16 Irvin D. Yalom and Molyn Leszcz, *The Theory and Practice of Group Psychotherapy,* 5th edition, (New York: Basic Books, 2005) 98-106.

Maslow's Hierarchy of Needs.[17] Maslow believed that all human beings are striving, and as a result, the goal of human development is to reach a point of self-actualization. Self-actualization is described as a growth-oriented motive that serves a powerful role in human development.[18] (See Figure 9.1) In Maslow's theory, the first level revolves around getting one's physiological needs met, which corresponds to Solomon's discussing food and drink (Ecc 9:7). The second level of the pyramid is safety, which includes having resources, security for the body, health, and family. Solomon describes his second group of things to enjoy as being related to comfort and clothing (Ecc 9:8). Maslow's third level involves resolving man's need for love and belonging, including family, friendship, and sexual intimacy whereas Solomon discusses the need to enjoy one's wife and the benefits of marriage. Maslow's final level prior to self-actualization is esteem, which involves one's achievements and confidence. The final area that Solomon lists for enjoyment is work, which he instructs man to do with all his might (Ecc 9:9). The similarities between Solomon's list and Abraham Maslow's show that man's basic needs have never changed.

What is the end goal of self-actualization, and does Solomon reach these same conclusions? The end goal for Solomon is the development of wisdom in how one lives his or her life. According to Abraham Maslow, the goal is to develop self-actualization. Maslow[19] believed that once the first four levels are achieved, people will feel compelled to reach their full potential as authentic people, driven to be very concerned about the interest of others.[20] Maslow was a humanist who had trouble late in his life understanding why more people didn't self-actualize after the first four levels were achieved. What Maslow failed to grasp as a humanist was the depravity of man, Solomon addresses this depravity when he states, "This is an

---

17 Barbara M. Newman and Philip R. Newman, *Development through Life: A Psychological Approach,* 11th edition, (Belmont, CA: Wadsworth Cengage Learning, 2012), 435.

18 Ibid, 434.

19 Ibid.

20 Ibid.

evil in all that is done under the sun that the same event happens to all. Also, the hearts of the children of man are full of evil, and madness is in their hearts while they live, and after that they go to the dead" (Ecc 9:3). Solomon illustrates repeatedly throughout Ecclesiastes the depravity of the human heart. He did not live under the illusion that human beings would do the right thing. Solomon seems to point to the notion that we should enjoy these four levels identified in Maslow's Hierarchy of Needs. However, we must appreciate God's gifts in light of the fact that we are sinful and selfish people. At the end of chapter nine we're left thinking that God wants us to enjoy His gifts in these four levels but not for the purpose of becoming self-actualized. Instead, is Solomon pleading with us to enjoy this very short, temporal experience, with an understanding to live a life of meaning "remembering death" because we don't know how long each of us will have on earth?

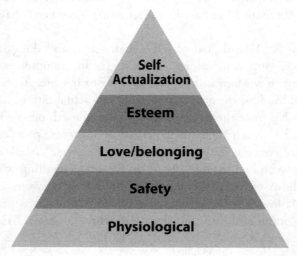

Figure 9.1

Ecclesiastes 10

10:1-7
The evil of foolish leadership

10:8-11
The evil of foolish living

10:12-15
The evil of foolish talk

10:16-20
The blessedness of wise leadership

10:1-7 The evil of foolish leadership

10:1-7 Dead flies make the perfumer's ointment give off a stench; so a little folly outweighs wisdom and honor. A wise man's heart inclines him to the right, but a fool's heart to the left. Even when the fool walks on the road, he lacks sense, and he says to everyone that he is a fool. If the anger of the ruler rises against you, do not leave your place, for calmness will lay great offenses to rest. There is an evil that I have seen under the sun, as it were an error proceeding from the ruler: folly is set in many high places, and the rich sit in a low place. I have seen slaves on horses, and princes walking on the ground like slaves.

In matters of life in general, and in matters of leadership especially, a little folly can do damage, just like a little dead fly can turn a pleasant perfume into a festering, rancid mess. Just as one can clearly see the difference between folly and wisdom, and between good-pleasing perfume and a stench, so one can clearly see the difference between a wise man and a foolish one. The wise man inclines his heart to the right, while the foolish one inclines his heart to the left. The word "right" here signifies skill and efficacy, while the word "left" signifies ineptitude and clumsiness."[1] The fool's folly is evident even in simple matters like walking down the street. As we walk through life, both the wise and the fool might encounter an angry ruler. If a ruler is angry at you, how do you respond? We are not told why the ruler is angry. The question is, "How should one respond?" Solomon's suggestion is to keep calm and not run. There is strength in one's composure and calmness.

As he is observing how things are "under the sun" (on the earth), he considers it evil when the ruler is a fool. We are assuming that this is not autobiographic. Or, is it? Does he recognize himself as the foolish ruler? Or, does he just recognize the truism that folly is present everywhere, even in the king's chambers? Regardless of what he means regarding the folly found "in many high places," why is it evil for the rich to sit in a "low place?" Garrett suggests that the word "rich" indicates not wealth but rather moral character.[2] Either way, Solomon suggests that it is not good to see "slaves on horses" or "princes walking." This reversal of the norm is seen as evil. Fox goes as far as saying that "the sages of Wisdom Literature, including Koheleth, were socially conservative. They condemned social injustices but did not envision or desire changes in the social structure."[3]

10:8-11 The evil of foolish living

10:8-11 He who digs a pit will fall into it, and a serpent will bite him who breaks through a wall. He who quarries stones is hurt by them, and he who splits logs is endangered by them. If

---

1 See Garrett, *Proverbs, Ecclesiastes, Song of Songs,* 334 and Fox, *Ecclesiastes,* 67. Krüger suggests right and left refer to good luck and misfortune. See Krüger, *Qoheleth,* 180.

2 Garrett, *Proverbs, Ecclesiastes, Song of Songs,* 335.

3 Fox, *Ecclesiastes,* 68.

the iron is blunt, and one does not sharpen the edge, he must use more strength, but wisdom helps one to succeed. If the serpent bites before it is charmed, there is no advantage to the charmer.

Starting with verse 8, the rest of the book will be composed primarily of "traditional wisdom sayings."[4] These are truisms that can refer to leaders or people in general. Digging a pit would not be a crime, but when its intent is for someone to fall into it, then it becomes evil. The teaching that someone's evil plans can backfire is not a new teaching; it appears earlier in the book of Proverbs: "Whoever digs a pit will fall into it, and a stone will come back on him who starts it rolling."[5] "Breaking through a wall" speaks of destruction of property in general, and one's safety in particular. The one engaging in such destructive activities might be met with the fangs of a serpent coming out of the rubble. Even if the activity does not have ill intent, one who "quarries stones" might be hurt by them, and one who "splits logs" opens himself up to the possibility of getting hurt. Fox correctly notes that "these mishaps are hazards, not certainties."[6]

Verse 10 speaks to the advantage of the wise worker who sharpens his ax, rather than uses unnecessary muscle power.[7] Verse 11 speaks to the disadvantage of the charmer who does not charm the snake before he gets bitten. Something that was supposed to bring him gain brings him "no advantage."

---

4 Garrett, *Proverbs, Ecclesiastes, Song of Songs,* 335. Ecclesiastes 12:8-10 is an exception. Bianchi argues against those who see this as the work of different authors. See Francesco Bianchi, "Qohelet 10,8-11: or the Misfortunes of Wisdom," *Bibbia a Oriente* 40.2 (1998): 111-117.

5 Proverbs 26:27. See also Psalm 7:16, 57:6.

6 Fox, *Ecclesiastes,* 69.

7 Frendo sees a broken construct chain here and suggests that the last phrase in verse 10 be translated "but the advantage of wisdom is success." See Anthony Frendo, "The 'Broken Construct Chain' in Qoh 10:10b," in *Biblica* 62.4 (1981):544-545, and Timothy J. Sandoval and Dorothy BEA Akoto, "A Note on Qohelet 10,10b," in *ZAW* 122 (2010):90-95.

10:12-15 *The evil of foolish talk*

10:12-15 The words of a wise man's mouth win him favor, but
the lips of a fool consume him. The beginning of the words of
his mouth is foolishness, and the end of his talk is evil madness.
A fool multiplies words, though no man knows what is to be,
and who can tell him what will be after him? The toil of a fool
wearies him, for he does not know the way to the city.

Wisdom literature is replete with language about speech. The book
of Proverbs has a lot to say about how the wise and fool can be quickly identified by their vocabulary and mode of speech.[8] Because the
wise is grace-filled, his/her words reflect that graciousness.[9] In contrast with the wise is the fool whose speech is not only detrimental
for those who hear his/her words, but these words "consume him."[10]
The merism (a figure of speech that employs two opposites to denote
the whole) "beginning of the words/the end of his talk" speaks of
the totality of the fool's speech. From the beginning one can see the
foolishness of the wicked's speech, and one can see that the end is
actually "evil madness."[11] Kidner suggests that the use of these two
words together points to moral and mental elements which are "the
final fruits of refusing the will and truth of God."[12] The fool is also
known for being verbose (Prov 10:19). His foolishness is tiresome
and is revealed by the lack of the simplest tasks, such as finding the
city, the best-known place in the area.[13]

---

8 Proverbs 1:6;12:18; 14:7; 15:2; 16:21, 23; 17:7; 19:1; 22:17; 23:9; 29:20.

9 The word can be translated "favor" or "gracious" and that appears throughout
the Old Testament to speak of God's favor and grace, or to speak of grace and
favor in general. Gen 6:8; Exod 3:21; Num 11:11; Deut 24:1; Ruth 2:13; 1 Sam
16:22; Ps 45:2; Jer 31:2; Zech 12:10.

10 Literally, "the fool's lips devour him."

11 This expression occurs only here in the entire Old Testament.

12 Kidner, *Ecclesiastes*, 92. He goes on to say, "If there are innumerable unbelievers
whose earthly end could hardly be described as either wickedness or madness, it is
only because the logic of their unbelief has not been followed through, thanks to
the restraining grace of God. But when a whole society goes secular, the process is
far more evident and thoroughgoing."

13 Pinker offers a reconstructed form of the verse to say, "The effort of the kesil in

10:16-20 The blessedness of wise leadership

10:16-20 Woe to you, O land, when your king is a child, and
your princes feast in the morning! Happy are you, O land, when
your king is the son of the nobility, and your princes feast at the
proper time, for strength, and not for drunkenness! Through sloth
the roof sinks in, and through indolence the house leaks. Bread
is made for laughter, and wine gladdens life, and money answers
everything. Even in your thoughts, do not curse the king, nor in
your bedroom curse the rich, for a bird of the air will carry your
voice, or some winged creature tell the matter.

The contrast between "woe to you"[14] and "happy are you" is clear.
"Woe" language is usually judgment language, while "happy"[15] is
usually language employed in blessings. People who are ruled by an
immature, decadent ruler should hear "Woe to you" echoed every
time the bottle of wine is opened and every time the clock strikes
midnight at the licentious party where the ruler banishes self-control. They are like "a fool when he is filled with food" (Prov 30:22).[16]
It is also implied in verse 17 that this ruler is given to drunkenness!
In contrast with the decadent ruler and his cursed subjects stands the
king who is "the son of nobility.[17] He has the wisdom to discern "the
proper time" for the feast, and thus knows how to exercise self-control, and preserve his strength for the affairs of the kingdom.

Verse 18 reminds all that slothfulness is not a spiritual gift.[18]
Rather, the lazy person's slothfulness can be readily seen as the roof

---

time will tire him, Woe to you, O city whose leader is as a child." See Aron Pinker,
"A Reconstruction of Qohelet 10,15," in *Biblische Notizen* 149 (2011):65-83.

14 The expression "woe to you" appears only here in Ecclesiastes with this spelling
and the second personal pronoun.

15 Deut 33:29, Ps 1:1, 2:12, 32:1, 40:4, 64:4, 84:4, 94:12, 128:2.

16 Fox, *Ecclesiastes*, 71.

17 This is the only place in the Old Testament that the expression "son of nobility"
appears. The word translated "nobility" can also be translated "free," or "noble
ones" in 1 Kgs 21:8-11;Neh 6:17, 13:17; Isa 34:12; Jer 27:20, 39:6.

18 Dahood finds in verse 18 three unusual pairs of words that are found in Ugarit-
ic. See Mitchell Joseph Dahood, "Canaanite Words in Qoheleth 10:20," in *Biblica*
46.2 (1965):210-212.

of his house collapses and the plumbing of the house falls apart. The industrious, on the other hand, earns bread and wine, so laughter and joy are part of his/her daily life. The one-liner "money answers everything" is not to be taken as a timeless principle. Rather, unlike the sloth, the industrious person can fix the leaking roof and plumbing with the money he/she earns.

The chapter closes with the warning not to curse the king or the rich. "Don't even think about cursing" the ones who possess political (the king) and economic (the rich) power concludes Solomon.[19] Fox suggests that, "This remark is a wry afterthought, as if Koheleth realizes that he himself has just insulted the king and the wealthy."[20] The wise person's speech is absent of curses and recklessness; rather his/her words edify and bless.

Reflections from a psychological perspective

In chapter ten Solomon expands on the benefits of wisdom as well as teleological movements and self-regulation problems associated with folly. There are several psychological theories which maintain that human beings are deterministic, and thus are people striving to satisfy biological drives. This is not the view of Adlerian Psychology which maintains that human beings are teleological beings. The term teleological means that an individual is purposefully moving toward his or her goals.[21] The term "goal" is best described as something we have control of, whereas a desire is something that we would like but we do not have control over.

Scripture repeatedly makes reference to the purpose or motive of our behavior and its implication in our lives (Proverbs 16:1-2, 20:5, 21:2, 24:12). In other words, we are goal-oriented people who act with a specific purpose in mind. Scripture teaches that we have goals in life that we want fulfilled but we must pursue goals that glorify

---

19 Thomas recommends the following translation, "Even in thy repose curse not a king, Nor in thy bed-chambers curse one of the rich." See David Winton Thomas, ""A Note on בְּמַדָּעֲךָ in Ecclesiastes 10:20," *Journal of Theological Studies* 50.199-200 (1949): 177.

20 Fox, *Ecclesiastes*, 71-72.

21 Manaster and Corsini, *Individual Psychology,* 5–6.

God (1 Corinthians 10:31). However, many people will come into counseling with a purpose or motive driving them that they are not aware of (1 Cor. 4:4-5; James 4:3). Many of these motives can be seen in the behaviors of our lifestyle, but they spring from our core beliefs about the world. Proverbs 24:12 states, "If you say, 'Behold, we did not know this,' does not he who weighs the heart perceive it? Does not he who keeps watch over your soul know it, and will he not repay man according to his work?" As we see in this verse, God knows both our thoughts and the motives for our actions. Adlerians therefore believe that one of the best ways to understand someone's actions is by first understanding what they want.[22]

If we are truly teleological in the pursuit of our goals, then how will the fool act as he pursues his or her heart? The person who is foolish in Wisdom Literature is frequently someone who speaks disrespectfully without grace and without thinking (Ecc 10:5, 7, 12-14, 20) and follows the ways that seem right to him (Prov. 26:12; 28:26). Thus the behavior of a fool is full of problems associated with his inability to self-regulate behavior. The term self-regulation refers to "how a person exerts control over his or her own responses so as to pursue goals and live up to standards."[23] The fools identified in Ecclesiastes walk in darkness (Ecc 2:14) often lack the ability to control their speech (Ecc 5:3, 10:12, 14, 20), and are prone to laziness (Ecc 10:18). Those individuals who struggle with self-regulation similar to the fool are not able to overcome their initial thoughts and emotional responses and thus fail to devise an alternate, more adaptive response. Baumeister et. al. conducted a comprehensive review of individuals who struggle with self-regulation and found correlations of substance abuse, gambling, sexual indiscretion, overeating, poor financial management, criminal behavior, and problems with anger and hostility.[24] This seems consistent with the problems of fools as noted in the book of Proverbs. Proverbs 21:2 states, "Every way of

---

22 Ibid.

23 Peterson and Seligman, *Character Strengths and Virtues,* 500.

24 Baumeister, Heatherton, and Tice, *Losing Control: How and Why People Fail at Self-Regulation,* 515, referenced in Peterson and Seligman, *Character Strengths and Virtues.*

man is right in his own eyes, but the LORD weighs the heart." The philosophical question is also raised whether self-regulation is genetic, a learned behavior (as many researchers believe), or a combination of both.

Does the believing brain change in such a way to aid in the development of more wise and self-regulating behaviors? Numerous studies show correlations with spirituality in children and adolescents and improved emotional regulation including less substance abuse and violence and a tendency to delay sexual involvement.[25] There appears to be evidence that into adulthood religiousness relates to less marital conflict, more consistent parenting, and improved relationships among all the family members.[26] Furthermore, it has long been understood that one's faith plays an important role in promoting prosocial values,[27] compassion,[28] and overall life satisfaction.[29] So if practicing one's faith seems to directly relate to improved or desirable behavioral outcomes, could there be a difference between the brain of someone who believes in God and the brains of those who do not?

A long understanding has existed that belief plays an important role in health and wellness, but we have always termed it the placebo effect. There is an impressive body of literature that emphasizes the role of belief in changing one's health, but could these beliefs pro-

---

25 Maton and Wells, "Religion as a Community Resource for Well-Being: Prevention, Healing, and Empowerment Pathways"; Stevenson, "Managing Anger: Protective, Proactive, or Adaptive Racial Socialization Identity Profiles and African American Manhood Development", 609, referenced in Peterson and Seligman, *Character Strengths and Virtues.*

26 Brody et al., "Religion's Role in Organizing Family Relationships: Family Process in Rural, Two-Parent African American Families.", 609, referenced in Peterson and Seligman, *Character Strengths and Virtues.*

27 Mattis et al., "Religiosity, Communalism, and Volunteerism among African American Men: An Exploratory Analysis," 609, referenced in Peterson and Seligman, *Character Strengths and Virtues.*

28 Wuthnow, *Acts of Compassion: Caring for Others and Helping Ourselves,* 609, referenced in Peterson and Seligman, *Character Strengths and Virtues.*

29 Ellison, Gay, and Glass, "Does Religious Commitment Contribute to Individual Life Satisfaction?," 609, referenced in Peterson and Seligman, *Character Strengths and Virtues.*

duce physiological changes to the human brain? The answer appears to be yes in a new field of study called neurotheology. In 1993 a study was conducted at the University of Pennsylvania, where they studied the brains of Franciscan nuns who had fifteen or more years practice in meditative prayer. These nuns were then asked to pray for forty-five minutes while researchers measured their brain activity. The researchers found that prayer was actively involved in regions of the brain associated with one's sense of self, emotions, and focus of attention. The results of this and other studies found that those who have a long history of prayer actually develop thicker and larger brains in the front lobe. The front lobe is involved in our ability to focus our attention, to concentrate on things, and to both control and regulate our emotions. So how does this relate to wisdom? Believers who spend their lives praying may actually have their brain changed in such a way that it increases their ability to self-regulate and to develop an improved ability to not respond impulsively. This improved self-regulation through ongoing prayer and conversation with God appears to physically change the human brain as wisdom increases.

Ecclesiastes 11

11:1-6
Be generous and industrious

11:7-10
Be responsible and joyful

11:1-6 Be generous and industrious[1]

11:1-2 Cast your bread upon the waters, for you will find it after many days. Give a portion to seven, or even to eight, for you know not what disaster may happen on earth.

The first two verses go together and they advise both generosity and wise investments. The Targum commentary of verse 1 emphasizes generosity, a concept widely developed in Wisdom Literature.[2] "Give your nourishing bread to the poor who go in ships upon the surface

---

1 Fredericks sees unity in 11:1-12:8 that can be shown through themes and rhetorical devices. See Daniel C. Fredericks, "Life's Storms and Structural Unity in Qoheleth 11:1-12:8," in *JSOT* 52 (1991):95-114. Contra Graham S. Ogden, "Qoheleth XI 1-6" in *VT* 33.2 (1983):222-230 who sees 11:1-6 as a "distinct literary unit."

2 Prov 3:9-10; 19:17; 21:25-26; 22:9; 28:27; 29:7; 31:20. See also Larry Magarik, "Bread on Water," in *JBQ* 28.4 (2000):268-270. Pinker suggests that there is an Urtext that reads, "Whisper your dream upon the water..." See Aron Pinker, "A New Approach to Qohelet 11:1," in *Old Testament Essays* 22 (2009):618-645.

of the water, for after a period of many days you will find its reward in the world to come."[3] The x, x+1 formula should not be taken literally, but rather as referring to both "generous philanthropy," and "prudent industry."[4] The German theologian Martin Luther recommended, "Be generous to everyone while you can, use your riches wherever you can possibly do any good."[5] The warning, "for you know not what disaster may happen on earth," points to the uncertainty of life, and thus one should act wisely with his/her resources.[6]

> *11:3-6 If the clouds are full of rain, they empty themselves on the earth, and if a tree falls to the south or to the north, in the place where the tree falls, there it will lie. He who observes the wind will not sow, and he who regards the clouds will not reap. As you do not know the way the spirit comes to the bones in the womb of a woman with child, so you do not know the work of God who makes everything. In the morning sow your seed, and at evening withhold not your hand, for you do not know which will prosper, this or that, or whether both alike will be good.*

As Solomon observed the way things happen under the sun, he noticed that rain falls when the clouds are full. Likewise, if a tree falls, it will lie there. The expression "to the south or to the north" is a merism. Wwherever a tree falls, it will just lie there. These images could speak to the inevitability of disasters and to the fact that humans cannot control the future.[7] Verse 4 returns to agricultural language. The farmer

---

3 E. Levine, *The Aramaic Version of Qohelet* (New York: Sepher-Hermon, 1978), 45. Garrett sees the verse as referring to overseas trade and diversification of investments. See Garrett, *Proverbs, Ecclesiastes, Song of Songs,* 338.

4 One need not create a false dichotomy between the two. See, Philip G. Ryken, *Ecclesiastes: Why Everything Matters* (Wheaton, IL: Crossway, 2010), 255.

5 Ryken, *Ecclesiastes,* 255.

6 Glasson is correct when he states, "Whichever interpretation we adopt of the opening words of Ecclesiastes 11:1 the general idea is clear, that the results of our action will surely emerge if we have the patience to wait until 'after many days.'" See Thomas Francis Glasson, "'You Never Know:' The Message of Ecclesiastes 11:1-16," in *EQ* 55 (1983): 43-48.

7 See Garrett, *Proverbs, Ecclesiastes, Song of Songs,* 338, and Bartholomew, *Ecclesiastes,* 337.

cannot wait for ideal conditions; rather, he must be faithful in sowing if he/she wants to reap. The farmer cannot be guided by observing the wind or paying attention to the clouds. Not only are humans incapable of controlling the rain and the wind, and thus incapable of knowing the future, but they also cannot fully comprehend what God is doing. Indeed, it is a mystery how "the spirit comes to the bones in the womb of a woman." Likewise, we "do not know the work of God who makes everything." Solomon was not an atheist or an agnostic. God was very real to Him even though he chose to disobey Him. Here Solomon affirms God's omniscience.[8] He does know when the rain will fall and He does know where the clouds go. The farmer is to be industrious. His/her job then is to sow the seed, to keep working "for you do not know which will prosper." Just as humans are invited to diversify when it comes to their money, here they are invited to diversify when it comes to work. In Wisdom Literature the wise is never portrayed as lazy; rather, they are industrious and diligent when it comes to work. The New Testament continues this idea when the Apostle Paul exhorts the believers to "work heartily, as for the Lord and not for men."[9]

11:7-10 Be responsible and joyful

11:7-10 Light is sweet, and it is pleasant for the eyes to see the sun. So if a person lives many years, let him rejoice in them all; but let him remember that the days of darkness will be many. All that comes is meaningless. Rejoice, O young man, in your youth, and let your heart cheer you in the days of your youth. Walk in the ways of your heart and the sight of your eyes. But know that for all these things God will bring you into judgment. Remove vexation from your heart, and put away pain from your body, for youth and the dawn of life are meaningless.[10]

8 Tsukimoto disagrees and calls Qohelet an agnostic. See Akio Tsukimoto, "The Background of Qoh 11:1-6 and Qohelet's Agnosticism," in *Annual of the Japanese Biblical Institute* 19 (1993): 34-52. Lohfink is also wrong in proposing a reader-response approach. See Norbert Lohfink, "Freu dich, Jüngling—doch nicht, weil du jung bist: Zum Formproblem im Schlussgedicht Kohelets (Koh 11, 9-12, 8)," *Biblical Interpretation* 3.4 (1995): 158-189.

9 Col 3:23.

10 In context, I believe the best way to translate the key word hebel is "transitory."

Solomon returns to the idea of joy.[11] Just seeing the light of the sun should prompt one to rejoice.[12] Yet, this joy needs to be tempered with the knowledge that in life one will also experience dark days.[13] Here, Solomon shows the contrast of life by employing light/darkness imagery. Indeed, these dark days will be many. This does not mean that Solomon is a pessimist. Rather, he is a realist. Life, indeed, is made up of good and bad days. The conclusion, "all that comes is transitory," seems pessimistic, but it is not; it is realistic.

Rejoice! That is the imperative for the young. But this is not a license to sin. Rather, this rejoicing is to be done responsibly, keeping in mind both God and the judgment day. This joy will be made up of things that one feels in the heart and things that one sees with the eyes. Kidner is correct when he asserts that "perfect freedom – must have a goal worth reaching, a 'Well done!' to strive for, to find fulfillment."[14] One way to ensure joy is to remove that which causes vexation[15] and pain.[16] "Joy was created to dance with goodness, not alone," Kidner says. The New Testament tells what to do when vexation wants to invade our life. The Apostle Paul writes to the church at Philippi, "Do not be anxious about anything, but in everything by prayer and supplication with thanksgiving let your requests be made known to God."[17]

---

11 Ecc 3:22, 5:19, 11:8.

12 Pinker suggest a different reading, "And sweetness – it's the light to the eyes, and good for seeing with sunlight." See Aron Pinker, "On Sweetness and Light in Qohelet 11:7," in RB 117 (2010):248-261.

13 Krüger argues that this refers to old age. Because days are shorter than long years, he holds that this refers to the period at the end of life when a man looks back over his life. See Krüger, *Qoheleth*, 196.

14 Kidner, *The Message of Ecclesiastes*, 99. Pinker suggests that 11:9-12:1 "deals with matrimony, advising young men about finding a spouse." See Aron Pinker, "Qohelet's Nuanced View on Matrimony: A New Interpretation of Qohelet 11:9-12:1a Within Its Pedagogical Milieu," in *Australian Biblical Review* 59 (2011):13-30.

15 This word appears in 7:3 and 7:9 and can be translated "sorrow, frustration, anger, or grief."

16 The word translated "pain" is the word "evil."

17 Philippians 4:6.

Reflections from a psychological perspective

Living life with the courage to be generous, faithful, joyful, and godly

At the beginning of chapter 11, Solomon encourages us to cast our bread upon the waters, which in essence is a reference to living generously despite the risks inherent in life (v. 1). Even within the psychological literature we see the benefits of living generously. One longitudinal study by Piliavin and Callero found that blood donors experience positive emotions from their generosity.[18] There is even evidence to say that teaching generosity through community service may decrease adolescent criminal activity[19] and may play a role in moral development, emotional balance, self-acceptance, self-esteem, social integration, and developing positive attitudes towards adults.[20] In Proverbs 19:17 Solomon states, "Whoever is generous to the poor lends to the LORD, and he will repay him for his deed," which may indicate that being generous actually produces its own reward. In fact one study suggested that the benefits of increased generosity could influence the psychoneuroimmunological pathways and consequently reduce mortality in aging adults.[21] It's easy in times of uncertainty to make excuses and to not live generously.

Solomon returns to the nagging realization that we have limited control. When faced with uncertainty, we tend to hoard our resources like we see in Ecclesiastes chapter 5, but this is not the instruction we get from these verses (3-5). Instead we are encouraged to live courageously, knowing full well that we cannot understand God's ways.

---

18 J.A. Piliavin and P.L. Callero, "Giving Blood: The Development of an Altruistic Identity" (Baltimore: Johns Hopkins University Press, 1991), referenced in Corey L. M. Keyes and Jonathan Haidt, eds., *Flourishing: Positive Psychology and the Life Well-Lived,* 1st ed (Washington, DC: American Psychological Association, 2003).

19 C Uggen and J Janikula, "Volunteerism and Arrest in the Transition to Adulthood," *Social Forces* 78 (1999): 331–62.

20 F.A. Newmann and R.A. Rutter, "The Effects of High School Community Service Programs on Students' Social Development: Final Report" (Madison: Wisconsin Center for Education Research, 1983).

21 D. Oman, E. Thorsen, and K. McMahon, "Volunteerism and Mortality among the Community-Dwelling Elders," *Journal of Health Psychology* 4 (1999): 301–16.

Solomon concludes that we cannot spend our time watching the wind, waiting to see where a tree may or may not fall, or waiting for the ideal weather to plant crops. We must accept the fact that we may or may not get the rain needed for our crops (vs.3-5), but this should not prevent us from living courageously. Adlerian psychology holds that courage is a core concept because human beings are goal-oriented and are either pursuing useful (right) or useless (wrong) behaviors.[22] Manaster and Corsini explain that courage "essentially consists of two elements: activity (rate of movement toward goals) and social interest. Consequently, the highly active person who has interest in others is courageous—ready and willing to act to achieve in terms of his feeling of belonging to others."[23] As believers, we are to be people who demonstrate courage. We need not be afraid or discouraged, since living in God's presence gives us the necessary motivation to live above our fear (Ezek 22:13-14, 1 Chron 22:13; 28:20; Deut 31:6-7) in safe assurance of our eternal security in Christ.

Solomon in verse 6 seems to be encouraging us to live faithfully by doing our work diligently and leaving the outcome to God. In essence we must accept the harsh reality that we have no control over the outcomes of many of life's events, yet we are still responsible for our own work and behavior despite all of the dark days that lie ahead (v.7). We cannot make excuses or let fear cause us to shift the responsibility for our actions to God or someone else (1 Sam 13:8-14; 15:12-26; Gen 3:8-13). We are responsible for our actions. Adlerian Psychology, known as Individual Psychology, states that we are responsible for acting in social interest and thus for right and useful behavior. Manaster and Corsini further state: "The natural consequences of social living make one chargeable for one's own actions. The pain and suffering that come from useless (wrong) behavior, from not facing one's responsibility and proceeding with courage are natural consequences of a person's mistaken goals. If you do not hold up your end in life, it will fall on your foot."[24] We see personal responsi-

---

22 Manaster and Corsini, *Individual Psychology.*
23 Ibid., 55.
24 Ibid., 56.

bility throughout the Scriptures, including the tasks that were given to Adam and Eve (Gen 3:16-19, 23). When we sin, we are sinning against God, and throughout Ecclesiastes we see repeated references for man being held responsible before God (Ecc 12:14). Solomon warns us that throughout our life we will make many choices, but we must remember the choices we make will be brought before God in His final judgment (Ecc 11:9).

Chapter 12

12:1-8
Remember your Creator

12:9-14
Fear God and keep His commandments

12:1-8 Remember your Creator

12:1-8 Remember also your Creator in the days of your youth, before the evil days come and the years draw near of which you will say, "I have no pleasure in them"; before the sun and the light and the moon and the stars are darkened and the clouds return after the rain, in the day when the keepers of the house tremble, and the strong men are bent, and the grinders cease because they are few, and those who look through the windows are dimmed, and the doors on the street are shut-- when the sound of the grinding is low, and one rises up at the sound of a bird, and all the daughters of song are brought low—they are afraid also of what is high, and terrors are in the way; the almond tree blossoms, the grasshopper drags itself along, and desire fails, because man is going to his eternal home, and the mourners go about the streets—before the silver cord is snapped, or the golden bowl is broken, or the pitcher is shattered at the fountain, or the

> *wheel broken at the cistern, and the dust returns to the earth as it was, and the spirit returns to God who gave it. Meaninglessness of meaninglessness, says the Preacher; everything is meaningless.*

The expression "Remember your Creator" appears only here in the entire Old Testament and introduces the poem in verses 1-8.[1] Kidner suggests that this remembering "is no perfunctory or purely mental act; it is to drop our pretense of self-sufficiency and commit ourselves to Him. Such at least is what Scripture demands of man in his pride or his extremity."[2] It is best to start in one's youth to submit to God since one has the entirety of his/her lifespan to serve the Creator. The days of old age are classified as "evil," and as days in which one has "no pleasure." This is definitely an employment of hyperbole, an exaggeration to make a point.

Verses 2-7 are a collection of figures of speech that describe what happens to someone in old age.[3] It's possible that Solomon is speaking from experience; he has seen his physical body deteriorate.[4] "I have no pleasure in them" in verse 1 fits with his "Meaninglessness of meaninglessness, says the Preacher; everything is meaningless" refrain. Is this the perspective we need to have at the end of life? Certainly not! Compare Solomon's pessimistic view with the Apostle Paul's godly conclusion, "I have fought the good fight, I have fin-

---

1 Fox calls 12:1-8 "the most difficult passage in a difficult book." See Michael V. Fox, "Aging and Death in Qohelet 12," in *JSOT* 42 (1988):55-77. For a survey of interpretations see Hans Debel, "When It All Falls Apart: A Survey of the Interpretational Maze concerning the "Final Poem" of the Book of Qohelet (Qoh 12:1-7)," in *OTE* 23/2 (2010):235-260.

2 Kidner, *Ecclesiastes*, 100-101.

3 Seow suggests that the poem "paints a picture of the end of the world, with the darkening of all the luminaries of the sky and every possibility of light (v.2), sheer terror even among the strong and dignified (v.3a), sudden cessation of life-sustaining activities and the anticipation of dashed hopes (v. 3b), the end of all economic activities and social intercourse (v. 4a), the noisy settlement of birds of prey in desolated human habitats (v. 4b), and panic in the thoroughfares (v. 5a)." See C. L. Seow, "Qohelet's Eschatological Poem," in *JBL* 118.2 (1999): 209-234.

4 See Barrick's Table of Interpretations for the recommended meanings of the figures of speech. Barrick, *Ecclesiastes*, 203-208. Fox helps us remain humble, "No interpretation of this poem is entirely satisfactory; none (including the one I will offer) solves all the difficulties." See Fox, *Qohelet and His contradictions*, 284.

ished the race, I have kept the faith. Henceforth there is laid up for me the crown of righteousness, which the Lord, the righteous judge, will award to me on that Day, and not only to me but also to all who have loved his appearing."[5]

Verse 2 uses creation language which included the sun, the moon, and the stars (Gen 1:14-19). Solomon knew well the creation account of Genesis, so Barrick is correct when he affirms that Solomon "demonstrates his awareness of the Genesis account and puts some of its concepts to work for him in speaking of the Creator and the approaching death of a human person, one of the Creator's created beings."[6] Using metaphorical language, verses 3 and 4 depict a house in decline; the house is the aging body that is approaching the grave. The "keepers of the house" probably represent the arms and/or hands. The "strong men" that are "bent" could be the legs and knees, and the "grinders," who are fewer and fewer, probably represent one's teeth, while the dimming eyes are described as "those who look through the windows."[7] One's hearing is compared to the "doors on the street" being "shut," and one's stomach failing to digest is compared to the low "sound of grinding." Bringing low the "daughters of song" could refer to one's loss of ability to enjoy music or to deafness.[8]

The "almond tree"[9] that "blossoms" is an image of white hair; the "grasshopper" that "drags" along could be the loss of strength in general or even impotence.[10] The "silver cord" could refer to the spinal marrow connecting brain and nerves. The "broken golden bowl" could refer to the brain, and the "broken wheel" could refer to the

---

5 2 Tim 4:7-8.

6 Barrick, *Ecclesiastes*, 199.

7 Garrett, *Ecclesiastes*, 341, Kaiser, *Ecclesiastes*, 120.

8 Garrett, *Ecclesiastes*, 341, Kaiser, *Ecclesiastes*, 120, Fox, *Ecclesiastes*, 79.

9 Moore suggests that the word might be the name of a vegetable. See George Foot Moore, "The Caper-plant and Its Edible Products: With Reference to Eccles. XII 5," in JBL 10.1 (1891):55-64.

10 Garrett, *Ecclesiastes*, 341, Kaiser, *Ecclesiastes*, 121, Fox, *Ecclesiastes*, 79. Youngblood recommends that "dark house" is a better translation than "eternal home" in 12:5. See Ronald F. Youngblood, "Qoheleth's 'Dark House' (Ecc 12:5)," in *JETS* 29.4 (1986):397-410.

veins and arteries.[11] Verse 7 is a reference back to Genesis when the Bible affirms that God made Adam from the dust of the ground (Gen 2:7). And even though Solomon believes in the Creator God, who is sovereign over both life and death, he concludes that everything is meaningless, all is futile.[12]

12:9-14 *Fear God and keep His commandments*

> *12:9-10 Besides being wise, the Preacher also taught the people knowledge, weighing and studying and arranging many proverbs with great care. The Preacher sought to find words of delight, and uprightly he wrote words of truth.*

The shift to the third person leads most scholars to believe that verses 9-14 are written by a frame narrator, and they represent the epilogue of the book.[13] Written by an unknown writer of great literary skill, the epilogue summarizes Solomon's resumé. Not only was he wise, but he taught people knowledge, and he wrote and arranged proverbs with "great care." Indeed, that was the modus operandi of ancient sages. The Chronicler of 1 Kings tells us that Solomon wrote 3000 proverbs and composed 1005 songs.[14] According to the epilogue, Solomon sought to find "words of delight" and wrote "words of truth." It is interesting that he said that Solomon "sought to find words of delight." Could it be that, like in other searches, Solomon sought but did not find such words?[15] Zimmermann argues that

---

11 Kaiser, *Ecclesiastes*, 121.

12 Anderson suggests that 1:2 and 12:8 "constitute a thesis/validation formula—which the two creation poems of 1,4-11 and 11,1-12,7 (along with 1,2 and 12,8)—form an inclusion to prove the thesis of *Qoheleth* that *hakol hevel.*" See William H. U. Anderson, "The Poetic Inclusio of Qoheleth in Relation to 1:2 and 12:8," in *Scandinavian Journal of the Old Testament* 12.2 (1998): 203-213.

13 Sheppard suggests that "the epilogue provides a rare glimpse into a comprehensive, canon-conscious formulation of what the purpose of biblical wisdom is." See Gerald T. Sheppard, "Epilogue to Qoheleth as Theological Commentary," in *CBQ* 39.2 (1977): 182-189.

14 1 Kings 4:29-34.

15 For an in-depth look at Solomon's search-to-find motif see Tiberius Rata, "The Seek-to-Find Motif in Ecclesiastes," in *Scripture and Interpretation* IV/2

12:10 was written by one of Qoheleth's disciple, and the words here represent an apology. This disciple "attempted to cover up Qohelet's deficiencies, who to the contrary, did not write pleasing themes (futility, death, self- deprecation), nor use an appropriate style (abrupt and frequently incoherent), or true words (questioned by traditionalists and rationalists)."[16] Scott suggests that the professional wise man who edited the book was an admirer of Qohelet but warns the reader against "being confused by the divergent and even daring ideas presented."[17] Keddie is among the few who believe that all that Qoheleth said so far is both upright and true. After all, "it has been a Word from God!"[18]

Did Solomon speak pleasing words and words of truth? I think not. Most of the time, he managed to speak neither pleasing words, nor words of truth. He sought to find them, but he rarely found them. His search proves again to be fruitless. Not because he was not wise, but because he chose to consistently and systematically disobey the God who appeared to him twice.

12:11-12 The words of the wise are like goads, and like nails firmly fixed are the collected sayings; they are given by one Shepherd. My son, beware of anything beyond these. Of making many books there is no end, and much study is a weariness of the flesh.

Verse 11 is a pastoral metaphor with God as the Shepherd. The words of the wise are compared to "goads." Garrett suggests that they "refer to the pointed sticks used to keep cattle moving in the right direction and so represent moral guidance and stimulus in human affairs."[19] The "collected sayings" parallel the words of the wise, and they are compared to firmly fixed nails. The image here attests to the foundation, firmness, and stability these words provide for the many complexities of life. Verse 12 is a warning that starts with the

---

(2010):151-160.

16 Zimmermann, *The Inner World of Qohelet*, 162.

17 Scott, Proverbs, *Ecclesiastes*, 275.

18 Keddie, *Looking for the Good Life*, 163.

19 Garrett, vol. 14, *Proverbs, Ecclesiastes, Song of Songs*, 344.

popular parent/child, sage/pupil expression "my son."[20] The warning is against going beyond the words and sayings given by the Shepherd. Ideas flow like water, so "of making many books there is no end." Solomon is not anti-academia or anti-knowledge. But when overdone, studying can be tiresome. The wise has to discern what to study and when to study.[21]

> *12:13-14 The end of the matter; all has been heard. Fear God and keep His commandments, for this is the whole duty of man. For God will bring every deed into judgment, with every secret thing, whether good or evil.*

Wise living is living in obedience to the Law of God. The commandments "fear God" and "keep His commandments" are not new. In fact, they originated in the Law with which Solomon's audience would have been well acquainted. After God gave His people the Ten Commandments through His servant, Moses, he encourages the people, "These are the commands, decrees, and laws the LORD your God directed me to teach you to observe in the land that you are crossing the Jordan to possess, so that you, your children and their children after them may fear the LORD your God as long as you live by keeping all his decrees and commands that I give you, and so that you may enjoy long life" (Deut 6:1-2).[22] Moses' successor Joshua uses the same language after the Israelites entered the Promised Land.

---

20 This expression occurs only here in Ecclesiastes, but occurs numerous times in Proverbs (7:1; 19:27; 23:15, 19, 26; 24:13, 21; 31:2).

21 Bartholomew might be right when suggesting that this warning was for the Jews who were tempted with the folly of Greek philosophy. See Bartholomew, *Ecclesiastes*, 369. Lavoie argues that 12:12 "is not by a second hand; it's rather an ironical text in which the author offers a self-criticism." See Jean-Jacques Lavoie, "Qohélet 12,12 ou l'autocritique ironique," in *Laval Théologique et Philosophique* 66:2 (2010):387-405. Shields posits that verse 12 "warns the reader against over-indulgence in the ways of the wise – making books and study – for, as Qohelet amply demonstrated – the end of such tasks is *hebel.*" See M.A. Shields, "Re-examining the Warning of Ecc. 12:12," in VT 50.1 (2000):123-127.

22 For a relationship between the Torah, Proverbs, and Ecclesiastes, see Gerald H. Wilson, "The Words of the Wise: The Intent and Significance of Qohelet 12:9-14," in *JBL* 103.2 (1984):175-192.

"Now fear the LORD and serve Him with all faithfulness," Joshua commands the people (Joshua 24:14). Solomon's father David uses the same language in Psalm 34:9, "Fear the LORD, you His saints, for those who fear Him lack nothing."

The concept of fearing God continues in New Testament times as well. Peter encourages the first century church to "show proper respect to everyone: Love the brotherhood of believers, fear God, honor the king" (1 Peter 2:17). As John sees a glimpse of heaven, he hears an angel say, "Fear God and give Him glory" (Rev 14:7). After all, the godly in the Bible are described as God-fearing men and women. This fear of God is not a paralyzing fear, but one that makes us stand in awe of Him and draws us closer to Him. The concepts of fearing God and keeping His commandments are inseparable. When we fear God, we will keep His commandments. In Deuteronomy 5:29 God says, "Oh, that their hearts would be inclined to fear Me and keep all My commandments always, so that it might go well with them and their children forever!" When we fear God we will turn away from evil. Moses encouraged the Israelites, "Do not be afraid. God has come to test you, so that the fear of Him may be before you, to keep you from sinning" (Exod 20:20). Solomon then stands as an example of how not to live. He did not fear the Lord, but sinned against Him. Job, on the other hand, stands as an example of a God-fearing man. The book of Job introduces him as a "blameless and upright" man, "one who feared God and turned away from evil" (Job 1:1).[23]

Verse 14 reminds us that God is not just the Creator but He is also the Judge! We were reminded of that in 11:9, "Rejoice, O young man, in your youth, and let your heart cheer you in the days of your youth. Walk in the ways of your heart and the sight of your eyes. But know that for all these things God will bring you into judgment." I believe that here verses 13 and 14 show that even though he is disillusioned, Solomon repents of his ways at the end of his life. "Fear God and keep His commandments" is his charge to humanity. He is not writing from the perspective of the man who feared God and kept His commandments, but he is exhorting everyone to learn from

---

23 Some Hebrew editions of Ecclesiastes repeat verse 13 after verse 14 "so that the book not end with a threat." See Fox, *Ecclesiastes*, 85

his mistakes. The wise indeed learn from the successes and especially the failures of others. I believe Garrett concludes it well,

> Seen in this light, to "keep his commandments" is not to behave with the self-satisfied arrogance of religious presumption, nor is it a nod to piety from an otherwise impious book. Rather, it is the deepest expression of humble acceptance of what it means to be a human before God. Solomon as the Teacher, in his address to his aristocratic colleagues, has anticipated perhaps the deepest mystery of the gospel: The just [or righteous] shall live by faith (Hab 2:4; Rom 1:16–17; Gal 3:11; Heb 10:38).[24]

Reflections from a psychological perspective

This chapter begins with the phrase "Remember your Creator" (Ecc 12:1), encouraging the reader to ponder God throughout one's life. Remembering God throughout life requires that we have a basic understanding of how memory works. The ability to remember information is generally made up of three components: encoding (how information enters the mind), storage (the process of preserving and recalling information), and retrieval (the process of accessing information coded and stored).[25] Because the brain receives millions of pieces of information, it is forced to develop a very concise perception of the world. This is done through multiple processes, but one of the most effective ways of taking in a large amount of data is through our sensory memory.[26] The use of our senses can help in the encoding of information and may serve a valuable role in long-term storage of information. Interestingly, in his descriptions in chapter 12:2-6 Solomon refers to three of our senses, namely hearing, touch, and sight, to describe the aging process. They are also the senses most commonly lost as one ages. If our senses are useful in memory, then

---

24 Garrett, *Proverbs, Ecclesiastes, Song of Songs,* 345.
25 Deborah M. Licht, Misty G. Hull, and Coco Ballantyne, *Psychology,* 1st edition, (New York, NY: Worth Publishers, 2014), 237.
26 Ibid, 236-237.

why does Solomon tie our eventual death into his descriptions? Is Solomon trying repeated references to our failing bodies and eventual death to drive his point home? Another effective method of learning and recalling important information is through pairing it with strong emotion. Few events in our lives cement things in our memories more than near-death experiences or going through a traumatic event. As we think of events like September 11 or the birth of our children, most of us clearly recall where we were and what we were doing on those days because so much emotion was paired with those events. But how do those functions work in the brain? The brain's limbic system plays an important role in human emotion. The systems' amygdala nucleus gets credit for its role in handling fear.[27] The hippocampus may also help in regulating our emotions to avoid extreme responses and assists us in long-term memory storage. So how does "Remember your Creator" relate to these passages? The reason for the strong memory is that the amygdala and hippocampus work together to let us know that these events are very important to us. As Solomon pushes the readers of Ecclesiastes toward living life with death in mind, these memories are more likely to impress themselves upon our minds and be more readily encoded, stored, and retrieved. Furthermore, as Solomon challenges us to fear God and obey His commands, he helps us begin to see how fearing the Lord will make us more likely to "remember God."

We can see that God in His Sovereignty has a divine timetable for each person's life (Ecc 3:11), but we also see that this world will never fully satisfy us. Personally, I love everything about summer, from the hot temperatures to the opening of baseball season, and I even enjoy mowing my grass until October. As I read Ecclesiastes, I see myself like the grass that comes every spring to my yard; it flourishes for a while and then it's gone. God perceives time very differently than we do because a day is like a thousand years in God's eyes (2 Peter 3:8), yet we know that God is everlasting to everlasting (Psalm 103:15-17). The time of my grass is short but that doesn't

---

27 Andrew Newberg, Eugene D'Aquili, and Vince Rause, *Why God Won't Go Away: Brain Science and the Biology of Belief,* 1st edition, (New York: Ballantine Books, 2001), 44-45.

mean I shouldn't work diligently at my yard. Instead, I approach my grass with the idea that I will enjoy the sun and the sweat of brow, for this season will be over quickly. Likewise, we are to work diligently for God (Col 4:5) and not lose heart. We are to see life as a gift and thus experience the benefits of this season of life before it is gone (Ecc 12:1-8). There will not be another chance to experience this gift and enjoy the vanities that this life brings, so we might as well enjoy the God-approved ones now.

As we embrace the final verses in Ecclesiastes, we get the sense that Solomon is summarizing the main points that he has been making from the beginning of the text and from Proverbs (1:7). Solomon challenges readers to live as if their time is short and makes the argument again that they must be subordinate to God in their thinking, starting with fearing Him (Ecc 3:14; 12:14; Proverbs 1:7). This requires a subordinate or reverent humility before God. As we fear God and understand Scripture it will help us by penetrating our hearts, and it assists us in replacing intrusive evil thoughts and the illusion of our own self-sufficiency (see Figure 12.1). Solomon's father David knew this to be true as he prayed for God to search him and see if there was anything in him that was offensive (Psalm 139:23-24). David's final words to Solomon before his death were to "walk in his ways" and to "keep his statues, his commandments" (1 Kings 2:1-4). God also instructed Joshua in similar manner.

> Be strong and courageous, for you shall cause this people to inherit the land that I swore to their fathers to give them. Only be strong and very courageous, being careful to do according to all the law that Moses my servant commanded you. Do not turn from it to the right hand or to the left, that you may have good success wherever you go. This Book of the Law shall not depart from your mouth, but you shall meditate on it day and night, so that you may be careful to do according to all that is written in it. For then you will make your way prosperous, and then you will have good success. Have I not commanded you? Be strong and courageous. Do not be frightened, and do

not be dismayed, for the LORD your God is with you wherever you go." (Joshua 1:6-9)

We also see this concept encouraged in 2 Corinthians 10:5: that every thought must be taken captive and made obedient to Christ. Similarly to 2 Corinthians, Solomon stresses obeying God which comes both from the knowledge of God and through a transformed heart. Figure 12:1 shows that fearing God starts at the thought level, and our obedience flows from our thoughts. Thus, we will be held accountable for our thoughts and relationship with God as well as for our knowledge and our behavior.

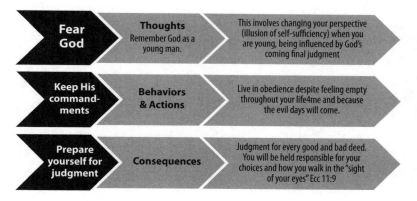

Figure 12.1